OKAY, I'M 80—NOW WHAT?

Finding God's Purpose for the Rest of My Life
Has It Changed?

ESTHER TITUS

ISBN 978-1-0980-4067-3 (paperback)
ISBN 978-1-0980-4068-0 (digital)

Christian Faith Publishing, Inc.
832 Park Avenue
Meadville, PA 16335
www.christianfaithpublishing.com

Printed in the United States of America

DEDICATION

*For my children, grandchildren and great-grandchildren
who I love with all my heart, and for whom I
consider it my purpose and privilege to pray daily:
Michael, Robin, Abbey, Ellie, Sierra Mercer
Rob, Shelly, Elijah, Breeze, Kail, Shiloh Titus
Zack, Rachel, Elliott, Pippa, Wilder Pittman
Brian Simmonds*

CONTENTS

My purpose will stand and I
will do all that I please.
—Isaiah 46:10

A PERSONAL JOURNEY

As a follower of Christ, I have a purpose in each day I live. What is that purpose? How do I find it? The Bible says to "call out for insight and cry aloud for understanding, look for it as for silver and search for it as for hidden treasure, then you will understand the fear of the Lord and find the knowledge of God. For the Lord gives wisdom, and from His mouth come knowledge and understanding" (Proverbs 2:3–6).

As I begin to write, one thought keeps coming to my mind: God's purpose did not change as I aged. His purpose when I left home to begin nurse's training at age nineteen was the same when I left Malaysia to marry Bob at age thirty-one. It was the same when my husband and I sent our children off to college in our fifties as when I moved to Alaska as a widow at age seventy-five. God was always purposeful in directing my life. He never fell behind, nor did He force His way to the front.

So what is new now? Nothing, really. As it relates to Him, my purpose is written in the pages to come: love Him, serve Him, watch for Him, and so on. It will only be adjusted according to my mobility, my capability physically, and even mentally, in how it is carried out.

The words on these pages are the result of my own digging into Scripture to see what God requests of me. It is my testimony regarding His leading in the past and my personal challenge to find God's purpose for the rest of my life. If the reader is encouraged or convinced by these words, I will be glad and God will be praised. With that in mind, perhaps it would help for you to read as though it was God's truth for you as well.

My purpose at the beginning of each day is to read God's Word and spend time in prayer. Each day to say, "Your will be done. Show me Your plan for today and I will follow. I am Yours. Take me, use me, as You will."

Follow, I will follow Thee, my Lord;
follow every passing day.
My tomorrows are all known to Thee;
Thou wilt lead me all the way.
—Margaret W and
Howard L. Brown

As I do what I know to do, the Lord will guide the next step, and then the next, one at a time. What I must do is open my heart and mind to Him. God knows me. He knows who I am and all about me. I just have to yield to Him and say, "Your will be done."

My husband Bob and I met at Biola University, and right from the start of our friendship, he would add the reference Psalm 37:4 and 5 (NASB), "Delight yourself in the Lord and He will give you the desires of your heart.

Commit your way to the Lord, trust also in Him and He will do it," at the bottom of each note that he gave me. This continued all through our marriage, with me writing the same on my notes to him. What we wanted above all was that we would never go ahead of God's plan for us, that God would make us want what He wanted, that we would delight in Him, and that we would commit our way to Him.

What is God's plan? "That in all things God works for the good of those who love Him, who have been called *according to His purpose*" (Romans 8:28–29). And who are those people: those who have been called according to His purpose? Everyone who has confessed that Jesus is Lord and has believed in his heart that God has raised Him from the dead (Romans 10:9). In other words, every Christian. I am saved to fulfill God's purpose.

LEARNING YEARS

God put me where I am right now, and He will use me right here—in this place, at this time, for one reason. My purpose is solely and completely to please God with my life, my conversation, my actions, everything. The next pages will help us discover how it is possible.

"God's purpose for you is not that you should be happy. It is to be Christ-like. This may involve pain and suffering, but joy can be in the midst of it." (Pastor Greg Kuehn*)

"You are my rock and my fortress. You are my hope. You are my confidence. You are my strong refuge" (Psalm 70:3–7).

---

* Dr. Greg Kuehn, pastor Sierra Bible Church, Reno Nevada from 1988–2014.

In the biblical account of Elijah running from Queen Jezebel in 1 Kings 19, was God in the wind, the earthquake, or the fire less than in the quiet voice? No. God didn't need a spectacular event this time to show Elijah His power. Elijah wouldn't have been able to hear Him. He was in no mood to listen. But God waited until He had Elijah's attention and then spoke quietly.

Has anyone been a teacher of small children? You will know from experience what I have only heard to be true: when the classroom is noisy, all the teacher has to do is speak more and more softly until everyone stops to hear what she/he is saying. There are times when God seems distant, and I wonder where He is. Maybe He's just waiting for my attention.

"Behold, I go forward but He is not there, and backward, but I cannot perceive Him; When He acts on the left, I cannot behold Him; He turns on the right, I cannot see Him. But *He* knows the way *I* take; when He has tried me, I shall come forth as gold" (Job 23: 8–10, NASB). I don't know where *He* is, but He knows where *I* am! He has me always on His mind. (See Psalm 8:4, Hebrews 2:6.)

"How precious are Your thoughts to me, O God! How vast is the sum of them! If I should count them, they would outnumber the sand. When I awake, I am still with You" (Psalm 139:17, 18).

As a child, I knew my purpose—grow up, learn what I could, practice what I learned, make a friend, be a friend, study, grow in knowledge, learn obedience, follow directions, begin to hear God's voice. He was leading me one step at a time and through the Holy Spirit speaking in my heart and mind, through His Word in particular.

I began memorizing scripture verses and feeding on them day by day through Sunday school, Vacation Bible School, and a wonderful Junior Youth Group that my parents taught.

For example, verses pertaining to my thoughts and speech, such as "May the words of my mouth and the meditation of my heart be pleasing in Your sight, O Lord, my Rock and my Redeemer" (Psalm 19:14).

And verses pertaining to my behavior, such as "Do you not know that your body is a temple of the Holy Spirit, who is in you, whom you have received from God? You are not your own; you were bought at a price. Therefore honor God with your body" (1 Corinthians 6:19, 20).

Through memorization of Scripture, I began to recognize certain responsibilities I had in growing up as a child of God. A children's song, for instance, applicable to everyone, expresses my need to be available for God's purposes:

I would like to tell you 'bout
a boy named David
Who herded sheep for his dad in Israel;
He wasn't at all precocious or significant,

14

But he grew up to be
King, the Bible tells.

Chorus: He was available for God to use,
Reliable, if God should choose
To take him and remake him
Into a vessel fit for the master's use.
And I want for Him to use me
In the same way, yes I do.
I want to be ready when he calls me,
Totally trusting him to see me through.

When Daniel and his friends
in far of Babylon
Were told they must bow down
to gods of wood and stone,
They prayed to God for
courage to be different,
And He used them for a
purpose all His own.
(They were available…)

Queen Esther was a Jewess
proud and faithful,
Her grace and beauty known
through all the land,
But when her people cried
out for deliverance
She didn't shrink from all
that God had planned.

(She was available…)

—EFT

At five years old I made the decision to pray and ask Jesus to forgive my sins. My Sunday school teacher led me to Christ, and I always think of that day as the point in my relationship where I gave Him my heart. It wasn't long after that day that a missionary speaker talked to this young girl's heart and she listened to God's voice about giving not just her heart, but her whole life to Jesus, as a missionary nurse to China.

Preparation for that commitment to Jesus included training to be a nurse. This meant moving to St. Paul, Minnesota, for nurse's training at Mounds-Midway School of Nursing, followed by a move to Los Angeles to attend Biola College (which became university) for Bible school.

Bob and I met one Sunday evening at Biola. I was asked to play piano, and when the "singspiration" was over, this handsome guy came over and leaned on the piano to chat. He ended up walking me back to my dorm, and that was that. Not long after meeting Bob and falling in love, my plans changed as I stopped hearing God's voice and listened only to my heart and emotions. My personal quiet time continued, though I only picked Scripture that had nothing to do with missions. Aah, but God…!

One morning, after getting off the night shift in the hospital, I opened the *safe* book of Psalms (no words like *commitment, missions,* or *dedication*) to chapter 55, down to verse 22, where I read, "Cast your cares (what He has assigned you) on the Lord, and He will sustain you." I couldn't do it alone, but with God's help I could obey Him and follow wherever He led. I realized anew that His plan for me was good and acceptable and perfect. God's love was ever and always in my heart. Now He was again settled on the throne.

Take my life and let it be consecrated,
    Lord, to Thee;
Take my moments and my days; let them
    flow in ceaseless praise.
Take my hands and let them move at the
    impulse of Thy love.
Take my feet and let them be swift and
    beautiful for Thee;

Take my voice and let me sing always,
    only for my King.
Take my lips and let them be filled with
    messages for Thee;
Take my silver and my gold, not a mite
    would I withhold.
Take my intellect and use every power as
    Thou shalt choose.

Take my love, my God. I pour at Thy feet
    its treasure store;
Take myself and I will be ever, only, all for
    Thee.

Take my will and make it Thine; it shall
    be no longer mine.
Take my heart, it is Thine own; it shall be
    Thy royal throne.
—Frances R. Havergal

I applied to OMF (Overseas Missionary Fellowship, the former China Inland Mission), was accepted, and sent to Chefoo School, the missionary kids boarding school in the beautiful Cameron Highlands of West Malaysia. Four years later God's plan brought me back to the US with a wedding dress in my suitcase and a wedding to plan. His plan for me changed, but His purpose remained the same.

Up to Now

Wherever you are, be all there.
Live to the hilt every situation you
believe to be the will of God.

—Jim Elliott[*]

To this point, I hadn't thought seriously or particularly about God's purpose for my life. I wasn't worried about what it might be, because it would always only be good. As Ecclesiastes 5:20 says, "(She) seldom reflects on the days of (her) life, because God keeps (her) occupied with gladness of heart."

I've lived beyond three score and ten, and a few years ago reached the big milestone of seventy-five. Looking back, I can see solid evidence of His guiding hand (call it His purpose, His plan, or His will) in everything I've done. Along the way there was the study of spiritual gifts, together with the love and desire for ministry, mostly in the music realm.

---

[*] Quote by Mr. Jim Elliott, missionary to the Auca Indians in South America and martyred for the sake of Christ, January 8, 1956.

Bob loved music and served as church organist for many years. We both played for church services during most of our marriage. To us it was ministry, as we accompanied the congregation, choir, small group, or soloist to the best of our ability as unto the Lord. As we played, we sang the words, either out loud or silently and worshiped the Lord. It was a joy, not a chore.

In 1 Chronicles 25 there is a wonderful section about David planning the music for the new temple that would be built by his son, Solomon. He set apart some of the sons of the priests "for the ministry of prophesying (maybe the musicians were also preachers!), accompanied by harps, lyres and cymbals…for the music of the temple of the Lord (v. 6) …All of them trained and skilled in music for the Lord" (v. 7). In addition, "Jeduthun…prophesied, using the harp in thanking and praising the Lord" (v. 3).

The musicians were appointed by family groups (along with their relatives)! What excitement there must have been in the homes of those Israelites. That is how Bob felt when he was invited to play the organ for a service, small or large. Just the joy of it was enough to get him through any rough days.

For our twenty-fifth wedding anniversary, the kids and I surprised Bob with an organ! The church he attended most of his life and where we attended for a while after our marriage was no longer using their organ and had it stored in a closet. That particular organ had much meaning to Bob, and I was allowed to purchase it very reasonably. My kids (plus a friend) made the four-hundred-plus-mile round trip across the mountains from Reno to California to pick it up, arriving home minutes before Bob's arrival from work.

Up until churches stopped using the organ (and sometimes piano) in Sunday services, we could both be found up front playing our hearts out to the Lord. When that era was over we felt lost, discouraged. What could we do now?

In Bible study I am again reminded to listen to the voice in my mind and heart. What is it saying? Is it a voice that encourages me and calms me? That is God's voice. Does the voice confuse me or discourage me or make me upset and rushed? That is the voice of the enemy. It is absolutely amazing what can happen when I stop and consider what is going on. A moment spent with head bowed and heart completely yielded to the Holy Spirit brings complete and joyful peace.

Thus, it was with my inability to focus. I had momentarily forgotten the key. The key is to let my mind dwell on what is "true, what is honorable, what is right, what is pure, what is lovely, what is excellent and worthy of praise" (Philippians 4:8, 9). When I stopped listening to the enemy and placed my mind on God and His Word, I came to the place of peace and assurance that a door of service would be opened, perhaps in another area.

By age seventy-five, I began to be intrigued with Acts 13:36 and King David's sense of purpose as a senior citizen *in his own generation.*

The five years from seventy-five to eighty have been learning years all over again. Learning new things and relearning old things. I've begun to understand what my purpose is now and to want to get going on what's next.

What to do today? Walk as a child of the Light (Ephesians 5:8–17). The fruit of the Light consists in all goodness and righteousness and truth, such as the following:

- Touch someone with God's love
- Make a difference
- Find out what pleases the Lord and do it
- Make the most of every opportunity

The verse in Acts says it this way: "David, when *he had served God's purpose* in his own generation, fell asleep." He died when he finished *serving God's purpose.*

When Christ was dying on the cross, he said, "It's finished." He had done what His Father planned from the beginning of time, no, before the beginning of time as we know it, before the creation of the world. *He had served God's purpose,* and it was finished.

God's purpose?

He came to die. "God so loved the world that He gave His only begotten Son, that whoever believes in Him shall never die" (John 3:16).

After all He's done for me,
After all He's done for me,
How can I do less than give Him my best,
And live for Him completely,
After all He's done for me.

—Betsy Daasvand

GOD'S PURPOSE FOR THE REST OF MY LIFE

As I read God's Word, I have become aware of what God expects of me now. It is not overwhelming, nor is it impossible, because He will help me do what pleases Him. My greatest desire is to serve God's purpose for the rest of my life, beginning with:

Acknowledge Me—"In all your ways acknowledge Him, and He will make your paths straight" (Proverbs 3:6).

Ask Me—"Ask and it will be given to you" (Matthew 7:7).

Believe Me—"I am the resurrection and the life; He who believes in Me will live, even though he dies; and whosoever lives and believes in Me will never die" (John 11:25).

Enjoy Me—"No eye has seen, no ear has heard, no mind has conceived what God has prepared for those who love Him" (1 Corinthians 2:9).

Follow Me—"If anyone would come after Me, he must deny himself and take up his cross and follow Me" (Mark 8:34).

Learn from Me—"I have learned to be content, whatever the circumstances" (Philippians 4:4).

Listen to Me—"Listen and hear My voice; pay attention and hear what I say" (Isaiah 28:23).

Love Me—"You shall love the Lord your God with all your heart, and with all your soul, and with all your mind" (Matthew 22:37).

Obey Me—"Blessed are all who fear the Lord, who walk in obedience to Him" (Psalm 128:1).

Pursue Me—"Pursue righteousness, godliness, faith, love, endurance and gentleness" (1 Timothy 6:11).

Remember Me—"Remember this… I am God and there is no other" (Isaiah 46:8, 9).

Seek Me—"Seek the Lord while He may be found; call on Him while He is near" (Isaiah 55:6).

Serve Me—"Be very careful to…love the Lord your God, to walk in all His ways, to obey His commands, to hold fast to Him and to serve Him with all your heart and all your soul" (Joshua 22:5).

Thank Me—"Give thanks in all circumstances, for this is God's will for you in Christ Jesus" (1 Thessalonians 5:18).

Trust Me—"Commit your way to the Lord, trust also in Him, and He will do it" (Psalm 37:5).

Watch for Me—"As for me, I watch in hope for the Lord, I wait for God my Savior" (Micah 7:7).

Worship Me—"Come, let us worship and bow down. Let us kneel before the Lord our Maker, for He is our God, and we are the people of His pasture and the sheep of His hand" (Psalm 95:6, 7).

ACKNOWLEDGE ME

Lord Jesus, make Thyself to
me a living, bright reality,
More present to faith's vision keen
Than any outward object seen;
More dear, more intimately nigh,
Than e'en the sweetest earthly tie.
—Charlotte Elliott*

Acknowledge Me. I am here. I am present with you. I will never leave you or forsake you. I come to bring peace to your heart, strength to your life, joy to your soul. Acknowledge My presence.

Webster's Dictionary describes "acknowledge" in several ways. Here they are listed by definition, followed by a truth from God's Word demonstrating that definition:

1. *To recognize as a fact or as one's own.*

---

* Poem written by Charlotte Elliott (1789–1871).

"No one who denies the Son has the Father; whoever acknowledges the Son has the Father also" (1 John 2:23).

2. *To admit as true or as pertinent; to confess as to acknowledge one's faults.*

"I humbly now acknowledge my transgression. Against You only is my sin" (Psalm 51: 3, 4).

God's response: "I will not look upon you in anger, for I am gracious, declares the Lord; I will not be angry forever, only acknowledge your iniquity, that you have transgressed against the Lord your God" (Jeremiah 3:12,13).

I love you. But I need to hear some declaration of guilt. I know you've sinned, but until you recognize that for yourself and confess your sins, I will not forgive.

3. *To admit the claims or authority of; to recognize*

"In all your ways acknowledge Him and He will direct your paths" (Proverbs 3:5, 6).

4. *To own with gratitude or as a benefit*

"All who see them will acknowledge that they are a people the Lord has blessed" (Isaiah 61:9).

5. *To own as genuine; to give it validity*

"Then I acknowledged my sin to you and did not cover my iniquity" (Psalm 32:5).

God's response: "You who are far away, hear what I have done; and you who are near, acknowledge My might" (Isaiah 33:13).

"I will go away and return to My place until they acknowledge their guilt and seek My face" (Hosea 5:15, NASB).

God is always ready and waiting for His people to turn from their sin and acknowledge that He alone can forgive their sins and save them. "I am the way, the truth and the Life. No one comes to the Father except through Me" (John 14:6).

Question:

"Then the word of the Lord came to Jeremiah, saying, 'Behold, I am the Lord, the God of all flesh; *is anything too difficult for me?*" (Jeremiah 32:27).

And another question, this time to Abraham:

"The Lord said to Abraham, 'Why did Sarah laugh, saying, Shall I indeed bear a child when I am so old?' *Is anything too difficult for the Lord?*" (Genesis 18:13, 14).

Answer:

Both Jeremiah and Abraham had to answer the same way:

"Ah, Lord God! Behold, You have made the heavens and the earth by Your great power and by Your outstretched arm! *Nothing is too difficult for You*" (Jeremiah 32:17).

"Yes, O Lord, I acknowledge You. You alone are life and truth, and to You alone I bring my worship. I acknowledge that in You I have everything that I need "for life and godliness through our knowledge of Him who called us by His own glory and goodness" (2 Peter 1:3).

Any relationship will suffer if there is no acknowledgement of a person's value, such as *pay attention to me*, or *I mean something to you*, or *I recognize you as important to me*.

One of my granddaughters, as a toddler, tried to follow and copy her big sister, but sometimes struggled to be heard. Then she would call out to anyone who was near, "Watch. Me." Pay attention. I'm here too. Other times she would say, "How about me?" As her grandmother, my response was, "Yes, precious, I recognize you. You are important to me. I love you."

Up to this point in my writing I have done a lot of thinking and praying about purpose, mainly God's purpose for me and how that differs from His plan and His will.

Plan—usually something we set in motion ourselves, without taking into account what God has in store. "Today I plan to do this or that. Please bless my plan, Lord," while all the while God is waiting for me to acknowledge Him, acknowledge that He is Lord, that I can do *nothing* without

Him (John 15:5). But I can do *everything* through Him who gives me strength (Philippians. 4:13). "I have been crucified with Christ and I no longer live, but Christ lives in me. The life I live in the body, I live by faith in the Son of God, who loved me and gave Himself for me" (Galatians 2:20).

Will—I will do this, or I will not do this. Again, it's often what I want, what I make happen. Instead we must say:

Not what I wish to be, nor
where I wish to go,
For who am I that I should
choose my way?
The Lord shall choose for me;
'tis better far, I know,
So let Him bid me go or stay.
—Charles Austin Miles

"Now listen, you who say, 'Today or tomorrow we will go to this or that city, spend a year there, carry on business and make money.' Why, you do not even know what will happen tomorrow. What is your life? You are a mist that appears for a little while and then vanishes. Instead, you ought to say, 'If it is the Lord's will, we will live and do this or that—'" (James 4:13–15).

"Be very careful, then, how you live—not as unwise but as wise, making the most of every opportunity, because the days are evil. Therefore do not be foolish, but understand what the Lord's will is" (Ephesians 5:17).

Purpose—What is God asking me to do? What is my purpose today?

I must have purpose: What I have in mind for today, is it God's purpose for me? Or is it just myself, my decision, my will doing something *on purpose* today.

In 1 Samuel 13:13 God said this to King Saul: "You have acted foolishly—the Lord has sought out a man after his own heart—because you have not kept the Lord's command. And after removing Saul, He made David their king. He testified concerning him: I have found David, son of Jesse, a man after my own heart; He will do everything I want him to do" (Acts 13:22).

"David, after he had served the purpose of God in his own generation, fell asleep" (Acts 13.36). He had a purpose. God had a plan for him, and he knew what it was. He wasn't perfect. He sinned, but the Bible says He was a man after God's own heart.

ASK ME

"I tell you the truth, my Father will give you whatever you ask in My name. Until now you have not asked for anything in My name. Ask and you will receive, and your joy will be complete" (John 16:24).

After Solomon became king, he "showed his love for the Lord by walking according to the statutes of his father David…" The king went to Gibeon to offer sacrifices, for that was the most important high place. It was "at Gibeon the Lord appeared to Solomon during the night in a dream, and God said, 'Ask for whatever you want me to give you.'" Solomon cites all that God had already given in making him king and making him ruler over His chosen people, "a great people, too numerous to count." And then Solomon asks for something that pleases the Lord: "So give Your servant a discerning heart to govern Your people and to distinguish between right and wrong" (1 Kings 3:4–9).

"God said to him, 'Since you have asked for this and not for long life or wealth for yourself, nor have asked for the death of your enemies but for discernment in administering justice, I will do what you have asked. I will give you a wise and discerning heart… Moreover, I will give you what you have not asked for—both riches and honor… And if you walk in My ways and obey My statues and commands… I will give you a long life."

My cat loves to be picked up, as long as it's her decision. I will know this because she will stand with her front feet up on my leg, as a puppy would. But if she hasn't decided it's time yet, she will circle my legs, then sit back and meow, circle, sit, meow, circle (all the time rubbing against me, getting more and more gray-and-white hair on my pants) until finally her front legs come up and I reach down to get her. When at last I'm allowed to pick her up, a deep purr can be heard. The answer has been there all along—she is going to want to be picked up—but she hasn't asked for it. I wait until the request is made, until she recognizes her inability to get there on her own.

Last year I made a trip by plane to the East Coast to visit my sister Margaret and her husband Dick. The trip required three different flights and three airports. I did well in Seattle, and in Portland, Maine, but the change in New York was one I hope to never repeat. Fortunately, there was a four-hour layover that I purposely arranged to give me time to get to my flight in a completely different location, different building, train ride, shuttle ride, elevators into the unknown. There were signs, but they often pointed to places I had just been, with nothing resembling the location pictured.

At one point, I saw a man in the Alaska Air section who looked as though he was closing his gate and might be able to answer a question. Approaching the harried man, I asked my question. He started to answer when my face must have registered unbelief, because he said quite angrily, "Do you want me to answer your question, or don't you?" I hastened to say yes, so he finished his explanation and I still had no idea what he was talking about.

When I finally was able to breathe after finding my gate more than three hours later, I started thinking about our gracious and compassionate Good Shepherd, who leads us in the way we should go, without being harried or distraught. The whole way, in answer to my continuous prayer for His guidance to one who could help, there was always someone—lovely people, every nationality, people rushing but willing to answer a question, people eating and willing to help. That was one day when I understood the Bible verse, "Pray without ceasing!" And as we saw before, "Acknowledge Him and He will direct your paths (Proverbs 3:6, KJV).

Sometimes God says, "No!" to my request. There is no doubt. He is very clear, and if I don't listen, there is usually a hard lesson to follow. Example from Scripture: In the first chapter of Deuteronomy, Moses is telling the story of the wanderings of the Israelites and how they refused to go into the Promised Land out of fear. They chose to believe the spies that cried, "We cannot defeat them!" So God told Moses to tell them to turn around and head back into the desert.

At the word they would have to go back the people repented and headed into battle with the Amorites, even though God said, "I won't go with you. You will be defeated by your enemies."

But in their arrogance, they rebelled against the Lord's command and marched up into the hill country. They "acted presumptuously" and went anyway. The Amorites chased after them and crushed them. "Then you returned and wept before the Lord; but the Lord did not listen to your voice nor give ear to you" (Deuteronomy 1:43). They presumed that God would help them as before. So instead of asking for His help, they went ahead to disastrous results. Our Father loves to be asked. "And I will do whatever you ask in My name, so that the Son may bring glory to the Father. You may ask Me for anything in my name, and I will do it" (John 14:13).

When I came to realize how God longs to be asked and how long He waits to be asked, I began thinking of all sorts of things to ask Him. What I discovered is that the answers are all in the Bible. When I read His Word every day and take time in the stillness of my quiet home to listen to His voice, the answer comes. It begins with "All Scripture is God-breathed and is useful for (*everything*)..." (2 Timothy 3:15).

During a heavy rainstorm my six-year-old daughter said, "Well, I guess God answered my prayer."

"Oh, what was that?"

"I prayed for rain."

All of a sudden there was a huge streak of lightning across the sky, followed by a loud thunderclap. As she grabbed my arm, Robin added, "But it sure is scary!"

Don't I sometimes ask for things and God sees fit to include a little thunder and lightning? It's not pleasant, but necessary, and I learn more about His power.

In Ephesians 6, following the section that describes the armor of God that all believers need to put on every day, comes this verse (v. 18): "And pray in the Spirit on *all* occasions with *all* kinds of prayers and requests." I put the armor on for my own protection and pray for others (see Psalm 23) for their protection from the enemy (vv. 4, 5); for spiritual restoration (v. 3); for freedom from want and need (v. 1); for peace in the midst of trials (v. 5); for comfort in pain and sorrow (v. 5); for guidance in walking the right path (v. 3); for a future with Christ in heaven (v. 6).

Jesus told His disciples a parable to show them that they should always pray and not give up. "He said: 'In a certain town there was a judge who neither feared God nor cared about men. And there was a widow in that town who kept coming to him with the plea, 'Grant me justice against my adversary.' For some time he refused, but finally he said to himself, 'Even though I don't fear God or care about men, yet because this widow keeps bothering me, I will see that she gets justice, so that she won't eventually wear me out with her coming!'"

"And the Lord said, 'Listen to what the unjust judge says. And will not God bring about justice for His chosen ones, who cry out to Him day and night?"

And the answer is a resounding yes.

BELIEVE ME

Do you believe Me?
Do you believe…

- that I am the Good Shepherd (John 10:14)?
- that I am the only way to heaven (John 14:6)?
- that I am the truth? the only truth (John 14:6)?
- that I am the light of the world (John 8:12)?
- that no one comes to the Father except through Me (John 14:6)?
- that I am the door (John 10:9, KJV)?
- that I am the Word (John 1:1)?
- that I and the Father are One (John 10:30)?
- that I am Life everlasting (John 3:16, 14:6)?
- that I love you with unfailing love (Psalm 33:18)?
- that I am the Resurrection and the Life (John 11:25)?
- that I am the Bread of Life (John 6:35)?

If you do, that is a good beginning. But our God is so much more. Remember what He said to Moses when he asked, "Who shall I say sent me?" when God called him to lead the Israelites out of Egypt. He said "I Am." Whatever you need, I Am. Wherever you go, I Am. Whatever you need to say, I Am.

What God says is true! He does not falter or fail. He keeps His promises. We need not fear that He forgets! If a month goes by, or ten years go by, and you still haven't heard from Him regarding the request you prayed for, remember that time, as we know it, means nothing to Him. He will answer…in His time!

"I trust in Your unfailing love; my heart rejoices in Your salvation. I will sing to the Lord, for He has been good to me" (Psalm 13:5). "Let the morning bring me word of Your unfailing love, for I have put my trust in You. Show me the way I should go, for to You I lift up my soul" (Psalm 143:8). "Blessed is she who has *believed* that what the Lord has said to her will be accomplished!" (Luke 1:45).

"I tell you the truth, whoever hears my word and *believes* Him who sent me has eternal life, and will not be condemned; he has crossed over from death to life…and the Father who sent me has Himself testified concerning Me. You have never heard His voice nor seen His form, nor does His word dwell in you, for you do not *believe* the One He sent. You diligently study the Scriptures because you think that by them you possess eternal life. These are the Scriptures that testify about Me, yet you refuse to come to Me to have life" (John 5:24, 37–40).

"If you do not believe that I Am the one I claim to be, you will indeed die in your sins" (John 8:24).

In the book of John there is a story of a "royal official" whose son was sick. In fact, he was "close to death." The official begged Jesus to heal the boy "before my child dies."

Jesus replied, "You may go. Your son will live." "The man took Jesus at His word and departed." Arriving home he found out that his son was healed at the exact time that Jesus said, "Your son will live." So he and all his household believed (John 4:46–53).

Later in John is a true account of *seeing is believing* and what the Savior thought about it. Jesus appeared to some of the disciples on the evening of that first Sunday after He rose from the dead, but Thomas wasn't with them. Jesus came to the disciples even though doors were locked, and showed them His hands and side. When Thomas heard about it, he declared, "Unless *I* see the nail marks in His hands and put *my* finger where the nails were, and put *my* hand into His side, I will not believe it" (John 20:19–20, 24–25).

"A week later Jesus' disciples were in the house again, and this time Thomas was with them. Though the doors were locked, Jesus came and stood among them… He said to Thomas, 'Put your finger here; see My hands. Reach out your hand and put it into My side. Stop doubting and believe.' Thomas said to Him, 'My Lord and my God!' then Jesus told him, 'Because you have seen Me, you have believed; blessed are those who have not seen and yet have believed'" (vv. 26–29).

Blessed are those who have not seen and yet have believed.

Do you believe in *Me?*
"Jesus said to (Martha), 'I am the resurrection and the life. He who believes *in Me* will live, even though he dies; and whoever lives and believes *in Me* will never die.'"

"All the prophets testify about Him that everyone who believes *in Him* receives forgiveness of sins through His name" (Acts 10:43).

"Repent and believe the good news!" (Mark 1:15). "We no longer *believe* just because of what You said; now we have heard for ourselves, and we know that this man really is the Savior of the world" (John 4:42).

"On the last and greatest day of the Feast (of Tabernacles), Jesus stood and said in a loud voice, 'If a man is thirsty, let him come to Me and drink. Whoever *believes in Me*, as the Scripture has said, streams of living water will flow from within him.' By this He meant the Spirit, whom those who *believed in Him* were later to receive" (John 7:37–39).

"But these are written that you may *believe that Jesus is the Christ*, the Son of God, and that by believing you may have life in His name" (John 20:31).

"For God so loved the world that He gave His one and only Son, that whoever believes *in Him* shall not perish, but have eternal life" (John 3:16). "Whoever believes *in the Son* has eternal life, but whoever rejects the Son will not see life, for God's wrath remains on him" (v. 36).

"If you confess with our mouth, 'Jesus is Lord,' and *believe in* your heart that God raised Him from the dead, you will be saved. For it is with your heart that you believe and are justified, and it is with your mouth that you confess and are saved" (Romans 19:9, 10).

"Who is it that overcomes the world? Only he who *believes that Jesus is the Son of God*" (1 John 5:5).

ENJOY ME

During my sophomore and junior years at Manual Training High School in Denver, I often rode the city bus to and from school. There were many students on board, including some from the Catholic school nearby. Several days I ended up sitting just in front of some of these students who were busy memorizing something, words that were familiar but not the context. Years later I recognized these words and phrases as part of the Westminster Catechism. I was completely mesmerized by what I heard and, in fact, memorized just by sitting near these Catholic students. One unforgettable sentence has become a comfort and a challenge through the years: "What is the chief end of man? Man's chief end is to glorify God and to enjoy Him forever!"

Glorify God? Certainly! I knew that every part of my life was to reflect and bring glory to the God of the universe, the God of my very existence, the God Who gave His Son to die on the cross for me. That was all part of my life and my belief system. I loved Him sincerely and supremely above all else.

But enjoy God? I pondered those words over and over. Yes, God was a good God, and I knew He answered prayer, and that He went to heaven to prepare a place for His children to live with Him one day. But He was so very holy, so above His creation, so beyond reach that I couldn't picture Him laughing, playing ball, telling stories around the campfire.

Slowly it grew in my mind and heart. This very God might be right now making a baseball field in heaven, putting in a huge swimming pool, collecting wood for a campfire, erecting a gazebo for morning coffee breaks with the patriarchs. I remember that in the story of Christ's birth, it was an angel from heaven, one of the angelic host that surrounded the Savior from before the beginning of time, who started the celebration, when he announced Jesus's birth to the shepherds. "Don't be afraid!" I have good news for you! News of great joy! Joy for all people! Not just a select few. Not just for the rich owners of the hotels that had no room for Him. All people. A Savior has been born *to you*! Leave your sheep. I'll watch them for you. Hurry to the village where you will find the baby (Luke 2:9–11).

Part of the wonder of God
Is the joy that He brings
To an ordinary day
Filled with commonplace things.

—EFT

"No eye has seen, no ear has heard, no mind has conceived what God has prepared for those who love Him" (1 Corinthians 2:9).

If that is true, which it is, we should be completely focused on that truth! Jesus told His disciples that He was going ahead to heaven to prepare a place for us! For us! He has been up there over two thousand years now, getting our home ready. With that in our minds, we should be having the time of our lives right here and now, with no room for gloom, no space for a sour face. I love Proverbs 15:13, "A happy heart makes the face cheerful." And "A cheerful heart is good medicine" (Proverbs 17:22).

No eye has seen,
No ear has heard,
No mind has conceived
What God has prepared
For those who love Him.
—1 Corinthians 2:9

As long as we are still in our mortal bodies, there will be pain and suffering around us and possibly in our own home, but as we look up to God, we can find strength and help to search for that joy that God has promised. The older we get, the harder it is to get our arthritic bodies to move, but God will meet us more than halfway and urge us onward in His strength, with joy…with cheer.

Motivations for this cheer:

"Your sins are forgiven" (Matthew 9:2).

"I have overcome the world" (John 16:33).

Now *this* is a party:

"On this mountain the Lord Almighty will prepare a feast of rich food for all peoples, a banquet of aged wine—the best of meats and the finest of wines. On this mountain He will destroy the shroud that enfolds all peoples, the sheet that covers all nations; He will swallow up death forever. The Sovereign Lord will wipe away the tears from all faces… This is the Lord, we trusted in Him; let us *rejoice* and *be glad* in His salvation" (Isaiah 25:6–8, 9).

Let's have a party; let's celebrate!
A sinner has been born again.
Send the invitations, open wide the gate;
Sing glory hallelu, Amen!
Glory halleluia, halleluia,

Glory hallelu, Amen!

—EFT

"There is *joy* in the presence of the angels of God over one sinner who repents" (Luke 15:10).

In the Bible story of the prodigal
son, found in Luke 15, we read
the father's joyful words:
"This son of mine was dead
and has come to life again;
he was lost and has been found."
And they began to celebrate…
Now his older son was in the field,
and when he came and
approached the house,
he heard music and dancing.
(His father) said to him…
"*we had to celebrate and rejoice*
for this brother of yours was
dead and has begun to live."

"For you who revere my name, the sun of righteousness will rise with healing in its wings. And you will go out and *leap like calves* released from the stall" (Malachi 6:2). "*Leap for joy*, because great is your reward in heaven" (Luke 6:23).

"The Lord is my strength and my shield; my heart trusts in Him, and I am helped. *My heart leaps for joy*, and I will give thanks to Him in song" (Psalm 28:7).

One day when my daughter was around four years old, we were stopped at a red light on our way to town when we saw a young girl on her way to school dancing around in one spot, completely oblivious to all the traffic. Robin watched for a minute and then turned to me with a look of complete astonishment. "Mommy, that girl isn't going *any* place!" She was having a private party and didn't care who saw her!

"You will *fill me with joy* in your presence, with eternal pleasures at your right hand" (Psalm 16:11). "There is a time for everything...a time to weep and a *time to laugh*..." (Ecclesiastes 3:1, 4).

"In Him we have redemption through His blood, the forgiveness of sins, in accordance with the riches of God's grace that He *lavished* on us..." (Ephesians 1:7–8).

Can you picture this? A huge dog races up the sidewalk, nearly knocking you down, and jumps on a man in uniform just returning from military deployment overseas. The dog slathers lavishly over the man's face in a profuse expression of welcome. His mouth is dripping in his excitement to see this man he hasn't seen in a very long time.

What a picture of God's grace lavished (bestowed profusely/squandered) on me. "How great is the love the

Father has lavished on us, that we should be called children of God!" (1 John 3:1).

One day I will see my Savior face to face.
When I meet Him I will not know how
to show my love for Him except to fall to
my knees in worship, unable to speak.

"Face to face with Christ, my Savior,
Face to face—what will it be?
When with rapture I behold Him,
Jesus Christ who died for me!

Only faintly now I see Him, with
the darkling veil between;
But a blessed day is coming,
when His glory shall be seen.

What rejoicing in His presence
when are banished grief and pain;
When the crooked ways are straightened
and the dark things shall be plain.

Face to face—O blissful moment!
Face to face—to see and know;
Face to face with my Redeemer,
Jesus Christ who loves me so!

Face to face I shall behold Him,
far beyond the starry sky;
Face to face, in all His glory, I
shall see Him by and by!"
—Carrie E. Breck

"We are children of God, and what
we will be has not yet been made known.
But we know that when He appears, we
shall be like Him, for we shall see Him as
He is" (1 John 3:2).

When I see my blessed Savior
on that peaceful shore—
Oh what a day!
Oh what a day that will be,
when my dear Savior I see!
In those mansions of love
now awaiting above,
Oh what a day, Oh glorious day!
—Unknown

FOLLOW ME

The story of Joshua being called by God to take over the leadership of the Israelites has helped me understand what it means to follow Him. We don't know exactly Joshua's thoughts on being made accountable for this heavy responsibility. But what we do know from reading Scripture is that they were about to take the final leg of the journey into the Promised Land.

Here's how it plays out in my imagination (From Joshua 1:1–9):

Now it came to pass that Moses died, and the Lord said to Joshua: "Moses is dead. He is with Me. So it's time to put off mourning, and rejoice instead. Get up. Rally the troops and get ready to cross this river!

You miss Moses. I know. But you need to remember that I put you in charge, and it's you that I will speak to from here on. I will not fail you or forsake you. Be strong and courageous. And be very careful to follow all that I told Moses. Don't look to the left or right. Teach what I tell you, meditate on what I say, do what I instruct you. No shaking in your boots. No giving way to discouragement. For the Lord your God is with you wherever you go.

> If things stay the same
> I will not run
> I will not fear.
> If things get worse
> He will see my through.
>
> —Unknown

One evening Bob and I were invited to dinner with a couple from our church. After eating, our host brought out a game which required us to take a card, read the question written on it, and answer it. When it was my turn, the question read, "What do you want to do with your life?"

My answer came as a surprise to Bob and, quite frankly, to me as well. "Be a writer." I was a registered nurse, had been to Bible College, spent time overseas as a missionary, but had not thought about writing more than the letters I wrote while in Malaysia. That started me wondering and thinking. Could I do something about that desire?

A Place for Everyone

There is a niche provided for every man;
Each makes his contribution
in God's great plan;
Let no one feel superfluous
in that vast scheme,
However small and hidden
his life may seem.

Some must go forth to battle;
some mind the camp;
Some cross the mighty billows;
some tend the lamp
And keep their lonely vigil
till break of day,
To guide some storm-tossed
vessel upon its way.

Some serve their generation;
some, those unborn;
Some lose their lives in
secret, like buried corn;
Some sow their fields with
weeping; some reap the grain
And fill their barns with
plenty from others' pain.

Dear Master, Thine appointments
to me are sweet,
If I'm but for Thy service a vessel meet;

In labors more abundant, or out of sight,
Thine openings and shuttings
are always right.

—Unknown

Not what we gain, but what we give measure the worth of the life we live.

It got me thinking about my spiritual gift. I wasn't completely ignorant of the subject, but only remembered some bits and pieces:

1) It was given at the time of my salvation.
2) It is something I already love or will grow to love after practice.
3) It may change in the way it's carried out through the years.
4) Often other believers who I respect will tell me what I'm good at.
5) It might be my talent.
6) Just because I'm gifted/talented on a musical instrument, for instance, doesn't necessarily mean that it's my spiritual gift.
7) I might have more than one.

Here are some Scripture references to read and prayer-fully consider (and there are many more).

"Each man has his own gift from God" (1 Corinthians 7:7). "Do not neglect your gift" (1 Timothy 4:14). "Just as each of us has one body with many members, and these members do not all have the same function, so in Christ we who are many form one body and each member belongs to all the others. We have different gifts, according to the grace given us" (Romans 12:6). Not only do we have a spiritual gift, but other gifts to go along with it—to be used for His glory. "For God did not give us a spirit of timidity, but a spirit of power, of love and of self-discipline" (2 Timothy 1:7).

We are to encourage, serve cheerfully, teach, give as generously as possible, govern in truth as God directs, all as unto the Lord. It's logical that my spiritual gift and my purpose are tied together, along with my particular interest. This gave me more food for thought and prayer.

All of us seniors, if we have been a Christian for many years, have most likely been using our spiritual gift in our churches most of those years. There is a temptation to slow down, to excuse ourselves, to let the young folk have the experience now—and the blessing. Because when we use our spiritual gift in the service of the Lord, it is a blessing... to ourselves and to the Body of Christ.

God's Word speaks to us in those moments of stepping back from, or stepping around, what God might be asking of us at this point in our spiritual journey:

1. *I'm not done with you yet* (Philippians 1:6). "Being confident of this, that He who began a good work in you will carry it on to completion until the day of Christ Jesus."
2. *My purpose for you is still active* (Psalm 138:8). "The Lord will fulfill His purpose for me."

3. *Keep it up* (Psalm 92:13–14). "The righteous will flourish. They will still bear fruit in old age; they will stay fresh and green."

I started making a list of people through the ages that served God's purpose in their old age. Look at these examples for instance:

- Moses was eighty when God called him to save his people.
- Billy Graham continued to write and speak into his eighties and nineties.
- Aaron began his work helping Moses at eighty-three.
- Abraham was seventy-five when he set out from Haran.
- Joshua was eighty when God called him to lead the Israelites into the Promised Land.
- Amy Carmichael was still at her post in Dohnavur Fellowship in India when she died at eighty-four.

We all know people in their eighties and even nineties who are still teaching Sunday school, mentoring young men or women, housing/ministering to missionaries on furlough, and more.

Every one of these people (and the list goes on and on) made a decision at some point to give his or her life to the Lord as a living sacrifice, holy and acceptable to God, *which was their reasonable service* (Romans 12:1). It wasn't out of line, or unusual, or an extraordinary offering. It was reasonable service. I pray that my life would be always offered to God in this way.

What I am hearing from some seniors is the sorrow that they are no longer "needed" to use their gift in the same way. There is a longing to be used in God's Kingdom and for His glory as before, but the place has been taken by younger people.

I often heard: *Fill a need.* But it seemed there was no place for me to play the piano. Everywhere I went there were wonderful gifted pianists. "What is it, Lord? Did you not give me this gift that I have used faithfully since childhood? What do you want of me?" At home I play faithfully nearly every day, trying to keep up my ability to sight-read. One day this phrase from Job came to mind: "The Lord giveth and the Lord taketh away. Blessed be the name of the Lord." I began to cry out, "Please, God, don't take this gift away."

One opportunity was presented, but someone else filled that need. What I thought would be a crushing blow was turned into praise. God has taken the pain away! As if to show me that He had indeed done it, one Sunday recently a lovely teenage girl was at the piano, doing a fantastic job playing along with the band. I could only praise God for releasing me from the pain and for giving this young woman a place in the church to do what God called her to do. He gave her a gift. It is her turn now!

During my life time there have been many moves—close by, far away, toward family, away from family, purposeful, unexpected. What I have found in thinking all this over recently is that each move has been part of God's purpose. Each move involved circumstances that brought joy or sadness to someone besides myself.

When I left Denver to attend school in Minnesota, it was hard for my parents. I was accepted to a local college, but God closed that door. Instead, He opened another more than one thousand miles away. God's purpose was not that I should get away *from* my parents and family, but away *to* the place I needed to be.

Sometime later, a huge move brought me across the ocean to the country of Malaysia, and then back to the US after four years. Not *from* that special place God had called me to, but *to* my marriage to Bob, because God knew my place was by his side. When Bob and I left Reno and all the friends we had made over twenty-five years, God's purpose was not that we should get away *from* Nevada but away *to* Montana. He knew what was ahead with Bob's diagnosis and death.

Other moves have been a part of life, but each one has been purposeful in God's eyes. There are times when God moves His child *from* a place that is not healthy, or is unsafe, and that is a move on purpose *out of* a bad situation. Always for a reason. One day, perhaps soon, I will make one last move—*from* earth *to* heaven, where loved ones are waiting. What a joy that will be!

You'll remain young and useful as long as you keep planning for tomorrow.
Never give up your dream. Obey God and leave all the consequences to Him.
(Author Unknown)

Many times I come to a standstill with a difficult problem where I can't seem to get an answer. It is at this point that I turn my eyes and my heart to my ever-present Lord with this verse from 2 Chronicles 20:12: "We do not know what to do, but our eyes are upon you." This situation takes place when Jehoshaphat was faced with an army of men from Ammon, Moab, and Mount Seir. The people of Israel were not going to be allowed to go through the land which God promised them. In reply, God gave them this promise: "Do not be afraid or discouraged because of this vast army. For the battle is not yours, but God's." All they were asked to do was to take up their positions, stand firm and see the deliverance the Lord would give them. Don't be afraid!

"Having done all, *stand*" (Ephesians 6:13).

If we say we are followers of Christ, we must live out that life. Discipleship is everything! "A student (disciple) is not above his teacher, but everyone who is fully trained will be like his teacher" (Luke 6:40). I am in training, and the Lord is my teacher.

Oh to be like Thee! Blessed redeemer,
This is my constant longing and prayer;

Gladly I'll forfeit all of earth's treasures,
Jesus, Thy perfect likeness to wear.

Oh to be like Thee! Full of compassion,
Loving, forgiving, tender and kind,
Helping the helpless, cheering the fainting,
Seeking the wandering sinner to find!

Oh to be like Thee! Lowly in spirit,
Holy and harmless, patient and brave;
Meekly enduring cruel reproaches,
Willing to suffer, others to save.

—Thomas O. Chisholm

My son, daughter-in-law, and eighteen-month-old grandson stood at the front door of our house, saying good-bye. They lived with Bob and me more than a year, and now their trailer is parked at the curb filled with their belongings, ready to move back to Alaska. With teaching certificate in hand, Rob's heart and dreams were full of the chance to teach school. Parting with the three of them doesn't come without pain. Oh, it hurts! As I hug Elijah, the tears are wrenched right out of my heart. You have been my sunshine for eighteen months. Where is it going to come from now?

"To you, O Lord, I lift up my soul. In you I trust, O my God. Do not let me be put to shame, nor let my enemies triumph over me. Show me Your ways, O Lord; teach me your paths; guide me in your truth and teach me, for

You are my God and my Savior, and my hope is in You all day long" (Psalm 25:1–2, 4–5).

Your ways.

Your paths.

Your truth.

Thank you, Lord. This is a good thing you are doing. How blessed we are to have children who follow wherever You lead.

In Mark 1:17 Jesus saw Simon and Andrew and said, "Follow me," and they did. No hesitation. *Immediately.* No questions. Then (v. 19) He saw James and John and said, "Follow me," and they did. *Immediately.* They left their father Zebedee in the boat with the hired servants, and went away to follow Jesus.

Later He saw Levi at the tax-collector booth and said, "Follow Me," and he left everything to follow (Mark 2:14). Finally, in Mark 3, Jesus went up on the mountain and summoned those whom He Himself wanted and they came to Him. He appointed twelve so that they would be with Him, and that He could send them out. He appointed, besides those five already picked, Philip; Bartholomew; Thomas; James, the son of Alphaeus; Thaddaeus; Simon the Zealot; and Judas Iscariot.

"They pulled their boats up on shore, left everything and followed Him" (Luke 5:11).

One more disciple was not one of the twelve yet was not afraid to make himself known as a Christ follower: a rich man named Joseph of Arimathea (Matthew 27:57). He didn't care who knew it, even going to Pilate himself to ask for Jesus body after His death. He risked embarrassment and ridicule to be counted as a Christian, one who was not ashamed to be associated with the King of the Jews in His death and burial. Along with Nicodemus, who visited Jesus one night (John 19:39), he wrapped Jesus' body in a clean linen cloth and placed it in his own new tomb that he had cut out of the rock (Matthew 27:59). Then they left. Their work was done. But in my mind I see these two disciples walking away heavy-hearted. I wonder how much they heard and understood about what was coming next.

The Bible says he (this Joseph) was rich. Another rich man came to Jesus and was told to sell everything he had and then come follow. "Jesus looked at him and loved him. 'One thing you lack,' he said. 'Go, sell everything you have and give to the poor, and you will have treasure in heaven. Then come, follow Me'" (Mark 10:21). There was a progression of instructions that day. Go...sell...give...come...follow. It was harder for a rich man to come to Christ. Harder than a camel trying to go through the eye of a needle (Matthew 19:24). But not impossible! Nothing is impossible with God.

This I know, that God is for me (Psalm 56:9). And this I also know, that I am for Him. But if I was a disciple of Jesus when He walked this earth, would I also have deserted Him the night He was betrayed? My heart says, "No!" But am I stronger than Peter was on that awful night? "All the disciples deserted him and fled" (Matthew 26:56).

Follow—to come after. "If anyone would come after Me, he must deny himself and take up his cross and follow Me. For whoever wants to save his life will lose it, but whoever loses his life for Me and for the gospel will save it" (Mark 8:34).

"This is to My Fathers glory, that you bear much fruit, showing yourselves to be My disciples. You did not choose Me, but I chose you to go and bear fruit—fruit that will last" (John 15:8, 16). What fruit? *Love, joy, peace, patience, kindness, goodness, faithfulness, gentleness, and self-control* (Galatians 5:22, 23).

That first Easter there were some very brief instructions given:

"Go," said Pilate, make the grave secure (Matthew 27:65).

"Go," said the angel, tell His disciples (Matthew 28:7).

"Go," said Jesus, tell my brethren to meet me in Galilee (Matthew 28:10).

"Go," said Jesus, make disciples of all the nations (Matthew 28:19).

When He says, "Wait," I trust
When He says, "Go," I must.

—EFT

To follow in Christ's steps takes courage. It takes courage to let go and let God take the lead. Sometimes courage is needed to just sit and wait. When Christ heads out, I want to be right behind, to be an encourager to those along the way. Many start out following, but the way is long and the path may be steep, so the *many* begin to lag behind. What a privilege to come alongside someone who needs a gentle nudge, a cold drink of water, and a word of encouragement along the way.

Recently, I had an amazing experience that highlighted what it means to come alongside in encouragement. I drove into Anchorage to watch two of my granddaughters compete in a swim meet. It turned out to be a time trial, to see if each individual swimmer's time on an event was in a competitive range enough to qualify for a big meet in a couple weeks.

The time went swiftly as swimmer after swimmer filled the lanes, with parents or other volunteers helping to clock the times. A special computer program also checked the moment the swimmer touched a pad at the end of the lane. Gradually, the swimmers and their families left the pool, their event over, and headed home.

Finally, only one swimmer was left in the pool, doing the butterfly stroke over and over, never slowing down, never looking around, his focus set. He was competing for a spot in a long-distance swim, one lap after another, up and back, over and over.

At the opposite end of the pool a fellow swimmer held a square waterproof board on which numbers could be changed to show the number of laps completed. Every time the swimmer approached the end of the pool, the teammate lowered the board below water level, just long enough for the swimmer to read the number: 50 meters, 100 meters, 200, 300, all the way to 630. 630 pool lengths, each one 25 meters long, for a total of one mile.

The very last time the board was lowered, it was covered with red tape, signaling the final lap.

The highlight of this event, in my mind, was the astounding support of three or four coaches on both sides of the pool yelling encouragement at the top of their lungs, walking quickly in pace with the swimmer, clapping, screaming out the words and cheers to let him know they were with him all the way. They never stopped until the swimmer was out of the pool. Tears were in my eyes as I thought again about the difference one encourager can make on life's journey.

In the Old Testament story of David fighting the Amalekites, "he fought them from dusk until the evening of the next day... Then David came to the two hundred men who had been too exhausted to follow him and who were left behind... Among David's followers were trouble-makers who said they would not share the plunder with these men. David's reply was "No, my brothers, you must not do that with what the Lord has given us... The share of the man who stayed with the supplies is to be the same as that of him who went down to the battle. All will share alike. David made this a statute and ordinance for Israel from that day to this" (1 Samuel 30:17–25).

"I have told you these things so that in Me you may have peace. In this world you will have trouble. But take heart! I have overcome the world" (John 16:33). "Be a man/woman of courage. Be strong" (1 Corinthians 16:13). You can, "because the Lord your God is with you, He is mighty to save." (Zephaniah 3:17). "Send forth Your light and Your truth, let them guide me; let them bring me to

Your holy mountain, to the place where You dwell" (Psalm 43:3).

Jesus calls me, I must follow,
follow every hour;
Know the blessing of His presence,
fullness of His power.
Follow, I will follow Thee, my
Lord; follow every passing day.
My tomorrows are all known to Thee,
Thou wilt lead me all the way.
—Margaret W. and Howard L. Brown

LEARN OF ME

"Whatever you have learned or received or heard from me, or seen in me—put it into practice... I have learned to be content, whatever the circumstances" (Philippians 4: 9, 11).

"Continue in what you have learned and have become convinced of, because you know those from whom you learned it" (2 Timothy 3:14). You know your teachers, your mentors. You know the example each of those people were to you as you grew in your faith and as you grew in your knowledge of God and His Word. They were unshakable in what they believed and taught you the same.

Learning is a process, no matter what area we are working on: patience, contentment, godliness, holiness, quietness, peacefulness, faithfulness. All require an attitude of resting in God and on His promises. "Learn to do right! Seek justice, encourage the oppressed, defend the cause of the fatherless, plead the case of the widow" (Isaiah 1:17).

Several years ago, driving back to Reno from the San Francisco Bay area, snow began to fall over Donner Pass, leaving the road sloppy with dirty snow. Cars and trucks passed, and soon the windshield was covered with the back-splash. The windshield wipers only made it worse. We had no choice but to pull over and try to clean it with a handful of snow. This helped, but only when we got to a gas station and cleaned it with soap and water was the window clear.

My mind was also clouded over with a spattering of jealous, fearful, anxious thoughts. There was a mental pulling over to the side to try to scrub away the grime with better thoughts, but it was temporary and didn't clear the *glass*. Only later, as I spent time with the Lord, and allowed God to wash me with water by the Word (Ephesians 5:20) was the fellowship restored.

Nothing between my soul and the Savior,
So that His blessed face may be seen;
Nothing preventing the least of His favor;
Keep the way clear. Let nothing between.
—Charles Albert Tindley

Waiting on the Lord

What opportunities God places in our lives to practice waiting. Instead of running pell-mell through life with no purpose, God puts obstacles, circumstances, opportunities in the way so we must stop or, at the very least, slow down.

If we are constantly seeking His will, His purpose, and listening for His direction, we are putting ourselves in the position for Him to show us the next step. Sometimes it's God's timing that we are waiting for. He hasn't said "no" but also hasn't said "yes," so we wait, expectantly. Not frustrated, not grumbling, but doing what life requires right where we are. It means not putting up a fight, getting ulcers, or making others miserable in our presence.

Who am I to dictate what God should do in my life? He has said very clearly that He is in charge. "For My thoughts are not your thoughts, nor are your ways My ways," declares the Lord. "For as the heavens are higher than the earth, so are My ways higher than your ways and My thoughts than your thoughts" (Isaiah 55:8).

"Wait for the Lord; be strong and let your heart take courage; yes, wait for the Lord" (Psalm 27:14). "Rest in the Lord and wait patiently for Him" (Psalm 37:7, 34). "Let the wise listen and add to their learning" (Proverbs 1:5).

In the book of Ruth I find a wonderful example of what it means to wait God's timing:

"In the days when the judges ruled, there was a famine in the land, and a man from Bethlehem in Judah, together with his wife and two sons, went to live *for a while* in the country of Moab" (Ruth 1:1). While they were there, the sons married women from that country and settled in. They became assimilated into the life and culture of the Moabites, yet longed for their homeland. In time Elimelech died, followed by his two sons. Naomi could not get the God-fearing Israelites, her friends, out of her mind and heart and decided to return to Judah, her homeland.

With Ruth, one of her daughters-in-law, she started back to Bethlehem. Ruth loved her mother-in-law and did what she could to assist in making a life after they arrived. Discovering that a close relative, a kinsman-redeemer, owned the field where Ruth was gleaning every day, Naomi began sensing God's hand in the situation. Boaz, the owner, was very kind to this foreigner, finding ways to give her more grain to carry home at the end of the day and encouraging her to stay in his field where she would be safe. Naomi recognized what Ruth must do and urged her to make use of an ancient custom to get his attention.

Ruth trusted Naomi and her God, who had become Ruth's God too, and was willing to do what was required to make her presence and request known to Boaz by going to his resting place in the night and spreading his blanket over her feet. He was very willing to be her kinsman-redeemer and set about making it happen. As the two women waited at home, it was hard to step back and allow God to fulfill His plan. I can picture the tension and excitement in their home as they waited for Boaz to return—Naomi and the lovely young woman who had become like a daughter to her. As Ruth waited anxiously, Naomi said, "Wait, my daughter, until you find out what happens. For the man will not rest until the matter is settled today." Or as the King James Version says, "Sit still my daughter, until you know how the matter will fall" (Ruth 3:18).

Wait...until you find out what happens.

Don't fret.

Don't wring your hands.

Present your need to your Redeemer, Christ.

Leave it there.

Don't try to rush God.

There is nothing to be gained by worrying the minutes away. There are things that need to be settled *outside* your situation in order to settle *your* situation.

This takes time.

But never too long.

"I wait for the Lord, my soul does wait, and in His word do I hope" (Psalm 130:5).

"Those who wait for the Lord will gain new strength" (Isaiah 40:31). "Wait for your God continually" (Hosea 12:6). "If we hope for what we do not see, with perseverance we wait eagerly for it" (Romans 8:25).

God is not in a hurry. I can take Him at His word and wait for His answer, His solution, His timing.

Look again at Joshua 21:45: "Not one of all the Lord's good promises to the house of Israel failed; everyone was fulfilled." What is different about those promises that makes them unrelated to the promises God has for us today? Nothing! He is faithful, just, trustworthy, and true. He will not fail.

Peace is not the absence of trouble but the presence of God.

—J. Oswald Sanders

"Do not be anxious about anything, but in everything, by prayer and petition, with thanksgiving, present your requests to God. And the peace of God, which transcends all understanding, will guard your hearts and your minds in Christ Jesus" (Philippians 4:6–7).

"Cast all your anxiety on Him because He cares for you" (1 Peter 5:7).

In your presence there is peace.
In your presence there is joy.
I will linger, I will stay
In your presence day by day,
That your likeness may be seen in me.

—Unknown

After moving from Montana to Alaska there was no opportunity to play the piano in a ministry position. A high wall seemed to be in front of me, blocking the way. Was God testing me? *I had passed the test many times in my life and come through fine*, I thought. Was this a trial I needed to go through to show my absolute willingness to do *anything* He called me to do? Maybe there was a new instrument I needed to learn. Maybe there was a new *place* I ought to be.

I tried playing for a nursing home, but they only wanted old-time popular music from years past, and I had never learned the melodies or words for many of these. Also, I had dedicated my piano playing to God many years before and understood it to mean I played for His glory, songs with words that honored Him, and I didn't want to veer away from this.

Maybe I should teach. Through the years there were always breaks in the need for a pianist, and in these breaks I usually found a Vacation Bible School or Sunday school class to teach. These were greatly satisfying days, and I loved the opportunity, but somehow always found my way to an old upright piano hidden in a corner of a basement or other out-of-the-way place.

Learning Must Never Stop

When we moved to Reno, our two children were in eighth and ninth grades, and I needed something else to do. Through the encouragement of my pastor, I applied for the job of church secretary. I was a nurse, mom, wife, and many other things through the years; but this secretarial job was the most challenging and fun way to earn a living. I loved it and stayed almost nine years, followed by nearly five years at the Meadows Bible Institute in Reno. This soon became Multnomah University—Reno Campus, and I only left because Bob and I moved to Montana.

My desire to become a writer became a reality in my acceptance to a correspondence course in writing from the Institute for Children's Literature in Connecticut. After five years of on-again off-again study, I received my certificate and filed it away "for safekeeping," never to be seen again…or at least for twenty-five years. I lost courage after receiving a couple rejection letters and decided that wasn't my niche, my gift.

After Bob's death from ALL (Acute Lymphoblastic Leukemia) in 2012 and my move to Alaska, I got my piano tuned and started to play again. But there was a problem. I was noticing a change in my ability to play. It was my habit to spend up to an hour a day playing piano in worship and praise, and it was getting more and more difficult. I couldn't do it. *If I lose this altogether, what is my purpose? Where will I fit in?* I wondered.

Now here I am, thinking again about purpose. A thought was beginning to form, a very strong message from God. I wouldn't think this way otherwise. "Get those stories out!" My stories and articles? You mean the ones in the bottom drawer? So I took them out, began putting them in some order, and worked on cleaning them up and rewriting parts that were definitely out of date. One by one they were redone.

I sent for a catalog of children's magazines with current addresses, editors, writers' guidelines, and other pertinent information. It was great fun getting some into the mail and receiving answers. Things were slow going, but amazingly I wasn't discouraged. If I was under God's headship, if He was really on the throne of my life, He would show me what to do next. In the weeks that followed, one story was accepted, and a small children's picture book was published.

That wasn't all. There were songs also. Songs that were written in the 1980s, 1990s, and early 2000s. Some had accompaniment and some did not. I did not show them to anyone in all those years. With God's prompting, and tons of His courage, I showed some to the children's choir director and she used one at Christmas. Since then I have spent many hours at the piano, and the music is coming back.

The most recent word plainly written on my mind and heart has been, "Write a book. Here's the name of the book, and here are the chapter headings." So here we go! *Okay, I'm 80: Now What? Finding God's Purpose for the Rest of My Life.* God gave me the message... *Do it!*

We have to take ourselves by the scruff of the neck and shake ourselves, and we will find that we can do what we said we could not... The Christian life is one of incarnate spiritual pluck. (Oswald Chambers, My Utmost for His Highest for May 20)

God, demand what You will, but supply that demand (From Psalm 55:22).

The point is not to keep busy for the sake of busy-ness, but to do what God has planned for me. There are many "busy" things in life that can consume time, but is that what God requires? Is it not to follow Him, learn of Him, worship Him? It is not, as a friend pointed out one Sunday while going over Proverbs 31, to be the *bionic Christian woman*, trying to do everything in my power.

As I learn more and more about Jesus and His incredible love for me, I'm beginning to open myself up to new things, most of which I always wanted to do but had never tried.

Sink or swim, said the instructor.
Are those my only choices?
No, you can float.
Floating is safe;
Floating is comfortable;
But you will go nowhere.

—EFT

LISTEN TO ME

Luke 9:34–35 Peter said to Jesus, "'Master, it is good for us to be here; let us put up three shelters—one for You, one for Moses, and one for Elijah.' (He did not know what he was saying.) While he was speaking, a cloud appeared and enveloped them, and they were afraid as they entered the cloud. A voice came out of the cloud, saying, 'This is My Son, whom I have chosen. *Listen to Him!*'"

You cannot love God and not listen to Him. The Bible is full of God's call to His people:

"Everyone on the side of truth listens to Me" (John 18:37).

"*Listen* and *hear* My voice; pay attention and hear what I say" (Isaiah 28:23).

"I gave them this command: Obey Me, and I will be your God and you will be My people. Walk in all the ways I command you that it may go well with you. But they did not *listen* or pay attention.

They went backward and not forward"
(Jeremiah 7:23, 24).

Those who choose to stop up their ears and not listen suffer the consequences of a life without the peace that
God will bring. When I remember to *hear* and really listen
to God through His Word, I have a completely different
life—one of the joy of obedience.

When listening to music, one thing that is very hard
to enjoy is music out of tune. Whether it's a voice, a vio-
lin, piano, or any other instrument, the listener becomes
fidgety, tries to plug his ears, or even leave the room if the
instrument is not in tune.

A friend told me this story, which is humorous, but
stems from the heart of a young man worried that his mom
would be the brunt of embarrassment:

She would often cover as a nursery substitute, but this
particular Sunday morning my friend wasn't needed. That
was delightful because she got to sit between her two young
teens for a change. As she told me later, the song was a
beautiful old hymn, and she was thrilled with the beauty
of the words and music. In fact it was filling her heart to
overflowing with joy, and about halfway through the second verse, she switched to the harmony. Her son looked at
her then leaned over and said very quietly, "Mom, you're
off key!" She could hardly stop giggling even in the telling.

"I will listen to what God the Lord will say; He promises peace to His people, His saints" (Psalm 85:7). His
sheep listen for His voice at the gate and "follow Him

because they know His voice" (John 10:4). "He calls them by name!" (John 10:3).

What joy to know the Savior, the Good Shepherd, well enough to recognize His voice.

In 1 Samuel chapter 3 is the account of God's call to the little boy Samuel. Thinking it was Eli calling, the child rose from sleep and quickly ran to the old prophet Eli. By the third call Eli realized it was the Lord, so he told Samuel to say, "Speak, for your servant is listening."

Speak, Lord. I'm listening.

"Samuel did not yet know the Lord; the word of the Lord had not yet been revealed to him" (1 Samuel 3:7). He didn't recognize the voice of the Lord yet; but out of absolute obedience, respect, honor and love for Eli, Samuel jumped up and ran to his priest. He had been taught to *listen,* and as soon as he *heard,* he ran to the voice.

Samuel was a little child who loved the Lord and learned to hear His voice.

He listened very carefully and followed Him for He was the Lord's own choice.

Samuel listened to the Savior's voice.

I am just a little child who loves the Lord and longs to hear His voice;

I'll listen very carefully and follow Him, for I want the Lord's own choice.

Listen to the Savior's voice.

—EFT

"Jesus called the crowd to Him and said, 'Listen to Me, everyone, and understand...'" (Mark 7:14). "Hear this, you foolish and senseless people, who have eyes but do not see, who have ears but do not hear" (Jeremiah 5:18–23).

Listen to Him!

For a very long time I wanted to own a grand piano (not a huge one, a small version) and presented it to the Lord as a wish in prayer request form. No demands, only wishful longing. Except it grew stronger and heavier on my mind. I thought about it day and night, never begging, but confidently asking as a daughter to a loving Father who knew her deep longing and would grant her request if it was good for her.

One morning, seated in the living room with my Bible open, reading and praying, I *mentioned* the matter of the piano. I felt my head turning to the side as the words came into my mind, "Look at your piano. What does it say on the cover above the keys?" I walked over to the piano and read, "Upright Grand" and out came an astounded "Oh!" as I burst out laughing. I *already have a grand piano*! This was an absolutely stunning discovery.

As with Elijah, I had been so busy...noisy...with my constant asking God for a piano that I hadn't taken the time to be silent. To listen...to wait for His voice. My one-sided conversation seemed to be, "Listen, Lord, I'm speaking!" May it never be true for any of us.

Within hours I phoned the piano tuner and asked him to give me an estimate on completely refurbishing the piano—gutting it and putting in all new felt pads, strings, and everything else contained inside the frame. The keys had been replaced once in its life and were fine. Everything else had to go. The estimate was less than a quarter of the cost of a used grand piano.

"One thing we have to get straight," he said. "There are two stipulations that must be met before I would even think of putting all that work into an old piano. One, the back must be free from any cracks which would weaken and make the piano not worth the bother. Two, it must have very great sentimental value." That it had. This piano, made by Becker Brothers in 1906, was purchased new for Bob's grandmother when she was a girl and was moved by train across the US from Canon City, Colorado, when the family moved to Grass Valley, California. It stayed in the family until Bob and I were married in 1970, and the piano became ours as a gift from Mom and Dad Titus. I loved the mellow sound right from the start, and we kept it tuned and well-practiced, even giving piano lessons on it for several years.

What a loving Father to give me exactly what was best. Not a new piano, but an old piano made new! I learned so much from this experience in prayer. God may say "yes" or "no," or even "wait," but He always answers, and it is always good.

I love the haunting sound of the wind chimes on a warm summer evening. It says, "Stop. Turn off the noise. Listen."

The breeze is gentle tonight as I write this, and as it passes, I wait to hear the chimes floating out in the air. Such a contrast to the insistent racket of the crickets. Much like the still small voice of God in our hectic rush-around lives. Stop. Listen. God is here.

Lately, I've been reading a book about the withdrawal of the China Inland Mission from China, *China: The Reluctant Exodus* by Phyllis Thompson and edited by M. E. Tewksbury. This mission, started by James Hudson Taylor in the mid-1800s, had grown to well over six hundred missionaries spread over the huge continent, plus a boarding school for the missionaries' children.

This book tells of the letters and cables that flew back and forth, warning of the escalating danger from the Communist Party. In the period around 1950 the danger to the local Christians was extreme and became more so as the months went by.

The Lord had a purpose and also a plan for its fulfillment. His purpose in reaching the Far East with the gospel never changed. The way to do that, the plan, changed. After much prayer and discussion, what came to be understood as God's plan was the continuing of the mission, but in different locations and with a different name, Overseas Missionary Fellowship. For a time, right into the years when it became my "family" from 1967–1970, we knew it at CIM-OMF until it was finally just OMF, with missionaries all across the Far East.

We yield to Him and say, "Thy will be done," and He shows the way.

The Surrendered Will

Laid on Thine altar, Oh my Lord Divine,
Accept this gift today, for Jesus' sake.
I have no jewels to adorn Thy shrine
Nor any world-famous sacrifice to make;
But here I bring within my trembling hand
This will of mine—a thing
that seemeth small,
And Thou alone, O Lord,
canst understand how
When I yield Thee this, I yield my all.

Hidden therein Thy searching gaze can see
Struggles of passion, visions of delight;
all that I have and am, and
fain would be—
Deep loves, fond hopes, and
longings infinite.
It hath been wet with tears
and dimmed with sighs,
Clenched in my grasp til
beauty hath it none.

Take it, O Father, ere my courage fail,
And merge it so with Thine own that

E'en if in some distant hour my cries prevail
And Thou give back my gift,
It may so changed, so purified,
so fair have grown,
so one with Thee, so filled with love divine,
I may not know or see it as my own,
But, gaining back my will,
may find it Thine.

—Morne Wallis

LOVE ME

One of my dad's favorite movies was *Fiddler on the Roof*. He seemed to feel a kinship with Tevye, though Dad only had three daughters as opposed to Tevye's five. After the two oldest daughters were promised to their sweethearts with the claim that they loved each other, Tevye began thinking about this claim to love, and this without the matchmaker's help. He came into the house one day to find out what his wife thought about this new self-served matchmaking skill.

"Golde, do you love me?"

Her shock finally gave way to a list of the ways she took care of her husband's needs: "I wash your clothes, I bake your bread…"

"But," said Tevye, "do you love me?"

She finally responded, "I suppose I do."

Then he replied, "And I suppose I love you too. It doesn't change a thing, but after twenty-five years, it's nice to know."

I was reminded of the conversation Jesus had with Simon Peter just before he was taken up to heaven. "Peter, do you love Me? Twice the question was asked, and the response was "Sure!" "Of course!" The third time Jesus asked quietly, "Do you love Me?" And this time the reply came just as quietly, filled with shame, remembering. "You know I do."

On November 30, 2018, Alaska experienced a magnitude 7.2 earthquake. I was seated at my dining room table reading my Bible having my *quiet time*. As the house shook and rattled with dishes shifting on the shelves or crashing to the floor, I stood in a doorway (remembered from my California days) and prayed that God would spare my house. It's a strange sensation watching the walls and floor undulating slowly and wondering what would be the outcome. Almost immediately after the main wave finished, one neighbor came running over to see if I was okay, and then another neighbor. Kindness not always experienced in this day.

One of my first thoughts after all was over was, *That's how I want to be found when Christ returns—loving Him, yearning for Him, studying His Word.*

When I thought about my kind neighbors showing their love to this nearly octogenarian, I realized that one of the ways I can purpose in my heart to serve God in my generation is to show that I love Him: unreservedly, constantly, with commitment, without fail, through hard times and good, closely, quietly, boisterously, gladly, in sickness and health—like the vows I made to Bob when we were married.

More love to Thee, O Christ,
More love to Thee!
Hear Thou the prayer I
make on bended knee;

This is my earnest plea: more
love, O Christ, to Thee;
More love to Thee, more love to Thee.

Once earthly joy I craved,
sought peace and rest;
Now Thee alone I seek, give what is best;
This all my prayer shall be: more
love, O Christ, to Thee;
More love to Thee, more love to Thee.

Then shall my every breath
sing out Thy praise;
This be the only song my
heart shall raise;
This still my prayer shall be:
more love, O Christ, to Thee;
More love to Thee, more love to Thee.
                    —Elizabeth Prentiss

"Because he has loved Me, therefore I will deliver him; I will set him securely on high, because he has known My name. He will call upon Me, and I will answer him; I will be with him in trouble; I will rescue him and honor him. With a long life I will satisfy him and let him see My salvation" (Psalm 91: 14–16).

No eye has seen,
No ear has heard,
No mind has conceived,
What God has prepared for those who
love Him.

—1 Corinthians 2:9

Loving Jesus can show itself many different ways. Not just the "cup of cold water" we give in Jesus' name or "something to eat" to one who is hungry. Not only visiting those in prison, or inviting a stranger into my home, or caring for a sick neighbor or family member, but doing whatever we do "as unto the Lord."

Two people in the Bible showed similar love and care for our Lord: Mary the mother of Jesus, after He was born, "wrapped Him in cloths and placed Him in a manger" (Luke 2:7). And Joseph of Arimathea "bought some linen cloth, took down the body, wrapped it in the linen, and placed it in a tomb" (Mark 15:46). Love in many forms, at the beginning and the end of Jesus's earthly life.

"You shall love the Lord your God with all your heart, and with all your soul, and with all your mind" (Matthew 22:37). "Hear, O Israel: the Lord our God, the Lord is one. Love the Lord your God with all your heart and with all your soul and with all your strength" (Deuteronomy 6:4–5).

"We love, because He first loved us… The one who does not love his brother whom he has seen, cannot love God whom he has not seen" (1 John 4:19–20).

"And this is my prayer: that your love may abound more and more in knowledge and depth of insight, so that you may be able to discern what is best…" (Philippians 1:9–11).

John 3:16

For god—the Lord of
earth and Heaven,
So loved—and longed to see forgiven,
The world—in sin and pleasure mad
That he gave—the greatest
gift He had—
His only son—to take our place;
That whosoever—Oh, what grace!
Believeth—placing simple trust
In him—the righteous and the just,
Should not perish—lost in sin,
But have eternal life—in Him.
　　　　　　　　—Author Unknown

Being retired was great at first. I was free—to clean house thoroughly, to sort old photos, to knit, to weed the flower beds? It didn't take long to finish those to-do lists. Then what? My siblings were busy in ministry. Every time I talked to them on the phone I heard "involvement" while

I couldn't even keep up weekly nursery duty because of painful joints.

For years there was constant action—worthwhile works, I thought. So now am I relegated to sitting on a shelf like a jar of peaches in Grandma's cellar? Poor me! I was beginning to sound like self-pity in its most destructive form.

One day God opened my eyes and I recognized it for what it was. I wanted the limelight! A place of importance, so that even if someone didn't recognize my face, they would immediately know my name and my title. When I was church secretary I knew almost everyone's name through church records, phone contacts, and pastoral appointments. Therefore, everyone recognized my name, if not my face. What God was asking of me was a yielded heart, a yielded life, faithfulness in small things. Show that you love *Me* above acclaim. More:

- Love and serve my husband
- Pray for my children and grandchildren
- Write or call another lonely person
- Listen
- Be an encourager
- Spend more time getting to know *Me*
- Keep a home where Christ is glorified
- Be ready at all times for who/what God might bring to my door
- Grow old gratefully

To love God is also to serve Him, in my home, in my neighborhood, in my family.

If our love were but more simple,
We should take Him at His Word;
And our lives would be all sunshine
In the sweetness of the Lord.
　　　　　—Frederick William Faber

In My Home

"Offer hospitality to one another without grumbling" (1 Peter 4:8).

My first Christmas living in Alaska, I was in the house I purchased just two months earlier. In fact, I got my keys from the realtor on my seventy-fifth birthday. This was the second major decision made without Bob. The first was to sell my house in Great Falls, Montana, after he died. It was a hard thing because I was happy there, and it was where Bob was buried. But with both my children now in Alaska it seemed wise to be close to them.

My son and his family live a short distance from me, up the Glenn Highway and off into the gorgeous forest up a turn or two where their log home and farm are located. My daughter and family moved to Fairbanks the summer previously. Before moving, they came to my house in Great Falls to tell me their plans and generously invited me to come with them. It didn't seem the right time, so I said I would wait a year before making that decision. As it turned out, their moving van had barely left the city when I called the realtor and put my house on the market!

One of my granddaughters flew from Alaska to help me pack and then back with me to Anchorage to look for a house. My ticket was a turnaround, allowing me the weekend to find a house I could afford. My son Rob came with me on this marathon, offering the guy guidance that I was missing so much. We looked closely at two houses, both needing repair and upgrading, but one was more *right*. So the papers were signed, and I went back to finalize the sale of my Montana home.

'Tis done; the great transaction's done!
I sold my house and 'm movin' on.

The buyer came, said "Yessiree,
This here's the house that's meant for me.

I like it, and I think I'll stay
And live here when she moves away."

So, I'll pack my bag and hit the trail;
Find a new address, and forward my mail.

It's excitin' times, don't you agree?

When God says, "Come. You follow me."
—EFT

Finally, I boarded the plane for my northward flight. Princess, my cat, did as well as any royal cat would, enduring plane changes and a long day. Once in Palmer, I had three days before the moving van arrived with my car and household furnishings. So Shelly (my daughter-in-law), her mom, and I set to work painting every room in the house. Anything else would have to wait.

In My Neighborhood

Because I had never moved into a neighborhood without my husband, it felt rather strange to be a "single" in a place where people seemed quite independent, content to spend the long days behind closed doors. What should I do? I like to know my neighbors. As a Christian, I need to be the one to open my door and go out to meet them—to take that first step.

A verse that came to my mind one day was 1 Samuel 6:1. It was God's message to Samuel when he was on a quest to find the next king of Israel. "Fill your horn with oil and be on your way." This was for Samuel, but couldn't it also be for me? My "oil jar" might be needed for soothing all sorts of bruises, hurts, damaged hearts, bullied spirits, loneliness. For a child, a single mom, a lonely widow, etc.,

God can lead us to an open heart who needs exactly your touch or mine.

Isaiah 61:3 says, "He has sent me to bind up...to comfort...to bestow...the oil of gladness instead of mourning, and a garment of praise instead of a spirit of despair."

With that in mind I began going on occasional prayer walks, praying for each home on my block, whether I knew their need, or even their name. Sometimes a knock on a door would be the beginning of a new friendship. I could show the love of Christ by my attitude and the repeated efforts to show what love looks like.

Now that I've been here a few years, I realize that I had formed an opinion without facts to back it up. One at a time I'm getting to know these wonderful people and have been able to share sorrow, joy, cinnamon rolls, apples, rhubarb, the promise of heaven, and more with these friends.

One Christmas, a couple years after moving to Alaska, I decided to have a Christmas open house. I sent invitations to come to my house on a Sunday afternoon during *Colony Christmas*, a happy celebration with decorated stores, a parade of lights, and fireworks. My seven Alaska grandkids came to help serve all the guests that were going to come. The *all* turned out to be eight adults (four couples, all close neighbors) and a two-year-old. We had a great time.

So the next year we did it again. My prayer this time was, "Father, bring someone who I can encourage, or who just needs a friend." Although no one came, I wasn't discouraged. That might not be the best approach for my neighborhood. I'm learning as God shows what to do next.

In My Family

"Above all, love each other deeply, because love covers over a multitude of sins" (1 Peter 4:8).

"I have no greater joy than to know that my children are walking in the truth" (3 John 1:4).

My parents were both born in Minnesota, met there (Dad's eye fell on Mom in the choir loft!), were married, and started their family. At the time my brother Brian was born in Minneapolis, things were changing in America. Jobs were hard to come by, and Dad had to go away from home to find work. Mom and Brian moved into her parents' fourteen-room farmhouse, and she went back to teaching in the one-room schoolhouse across the field.

The bedrock of Mom and Dad's life was faith in the God who would not fail. Mother had many memories of her grandparents in their apartment at one end of the farmhouse. She would often find her grandfather sitting at the kitchen table with his Bible open, in prayer. He prayed for his children, his grandchildren, and for the generations to come, that they would find Christ and become God's ministers into the world. God answered those prayers, as several in the following generations became ministers, missionaries, Christian workers, serving the Lord around the world.

My heritage is rich. "Lead me to the rock that is higher than I. For You have been my refuge, a strong tower against the foe... I take refuge in the shelter of Your wings. For You have given me the heritage of those who fear Your name" (Psalm 61:2–5).

"Your statutes are my heritage forever; they are the joy of my heart" (Psalm 119:111). "Surely I have a delightful inheritance" (Psalm 16:6).

Grandchildren—"Children are a reward from the Lord" (Psalm 127:3).

I have some fantastic grandkids. Ten to be exact (including a grandson-in-law) and three great-grands. My love for them is individual and total, each and all. They can't do enough to make me love them more or do anything to make me love them less.

Are my grandchildren and great-grandchildren going to meet me in glory? That is my daily prayer and probably my greatest purpose. Nothing is more important. The more time I can spend with them the better. We have all heard the true expression: God has no grandchildren, and I cannot wish them into the Kingdom. Nor can I love them enough. But by my love I can show them Jesus and His great love for them. Bottom-line? I don't want to enter heaven's gate without every last one of them.

> For mercies so great,
> what return can I make
> for mercies so constant and sure;

I'll love Him,
I'll serve Him
with all that I have
as long as my life shall endure.
—Thomas A. Chisholm

OBEY ME

On a walk recently I noticed a new sign posted along some road construction: "Do not enter." Then there was the "Stop" sign at the intersection and "Do not walk" by a freshly cemented sidewalk. Notices placed in specific locations for specific reasons. Obey the warning signs. Be careful.

What if I visit the doctor and find that my blood pressure or cholesterol is not in a healthy zone. He might recommend that I get more exercise or cut certain things from my diet for my health and total well-being.

Neither of these warnings is pleasant. They interfere with my life; and I would like to ignore the fact that they are given to help me live safe, happy, and healthy. If I choose not to obey, consequences will surely follow.

The Bible tells us some things for our good also. They are called commandments. "The Lord will again delight in you and make you prosperous, *if you obey* the Lord your God *and keep* His commands...*and turn* to the Lord your God with all your heart and with all your soul" (Deuteronomy 30:10).

"The Israelites had moved about in the desert forty years until all the men who were of military age when they left Egypt had died, since they had not obeyed the Lord" (Joshua 5:6).

Now they are facing a raging river, and God has hard instructions. He is asking them to walk straight ahead into the Jordan River. Yes, it's flowing fiercely right now, and the water is murky and dark. But no, they are not to wait until things slow down and the flood abates. That happened with Noah, not here. They are to pack up their tent, fold up their belongings, take their children's hands and get in line. God did not promise to make a way through the water while they're waiting around for things to look better. His command is to "Take Me at My word, walk right up to the river, step in and *then* they'll see what I will do."

Full obedience, and not half,
is what God requires.
Delayed obedience is disobedience.
Disobedience is sin.

"This is what the Lord says—your Redeemer, the Holy One of Israel: I am the Lord your God, Who teaches you… Who directs you… If only you had paid attention to My commands, your peace would have been like a river…" (Isaiah 48:17, 18).

Beware of reasoning about
God's Word—obey it.
—Oswald Chambers

Trusting and following Christ are part of learning to obey. "Although He was a Son, He (Jesus Christ) learned obedience from what He suffered" (Hebrews 5:8). "(He) became obedient to death—even death on a cross!" (Philippians 2:8). As God's child, I am learning to obey, as well as trust the One to whom obedience is given. This is not easy. It is a learning process—following through until completion whatever He has ordered.

I said, "Let me walk in the field";
God said, "No, walk in the town";
I said, "There are no flowers there";
He said, "No flowers, but a crown."

I said, "But the sky is black,
There is nothing but noise and din";
But He wept as He sent me back,
"There is more," He said, "there is sin."

I said, "But the air is thick,
And smog is veiling the sun";
He answered, "Yet souls are sick,
And your work is yet undone."

I said, "I will miss the light,
And friends will miss me, they say";
He answered me, "Choose tonight,
If I am to miss you, or they."

I pleaded for time to be given;
He said, "Is it hard to decide?
It will not seem hard in Heaven
To have followed the steps
of your Guide."

I cast one look at the field,
Then set my face to the town;
He said, "My child, do you yield?
Will you leave the flowers for the crown?"

Then into His hand went mine,
And into my heart came He;
And I walk in a light Divine,
The path I had feared to see.
—George MacDonald

In the book of Acts, Philip, a deacon in the early church who was present when Stephen was killed, was among the apostles scattered throughout Judea and Samaria because of severe persecution. Philip went preaching and working miracles, healing the sick and casting out evil spirits. Busy with the Father's work, he was given a message: "Go south." So he went. On the way he found an Ethiopian eunuch, an important official in charge of all the treasury of Candace, queen of the Ethiopians, in his chariot reading the book of Isaiah but without understanding.

The Spirit said to Philip, "Go to the chariot." So he *ran up*. No hesitation. No lingering. Immediate obedience.

And in the next moments he began at that very passage of Scripture to tell him the good news about Jesus.

The Israelites had a problem with obedience. It seemed so simple. An order was given, the order was obeyed, success was achieved, and a reward was promised. But many times the order was given, a blessing was promised, but the order was never completed or was carried out with so much grumbling and complaining that Moses threw up his hands and threatened to quit or God said, "Enough! I've had it!" It may have seemed simple, but I call it the complexity of simplicity. One order but too many participants. Too many people, each with their own ideas of how to comply.

God said, "If you obey, I will shower you with blessing like you have never known" (Deuteronomy 28:1–10). What was their answer? It's too hot. It's too heavy. I'm hungry. He/she makes me do all the work. The lesson was not learned. The people had to keep walking around Mt. Sinai until they learned it the hard way.

In 1 Chronicles 13 and 15, King David was enjoying victory in battle, watching valiant warriors by the thousands join his ranks. It was time to bring the ark of God back to Jerusalem. The whole assembly agreed to do this. So they moved the ark of God from Abinadab's house on a *new cart*, with two Israelites, Uzzah and Ahio, guiding it. When the oxen stumbled, Uzzah reached out his hand to steady it and the Lord struck and killed him.

David was angry at God's action, and he "was afraid of God that day" (13:12). So instead of bringing the ark with him, he took it to the house of Obed-Edom where it remained for three months. When it was time to bring back the ark, it was done "as Moses commanded in accordance with the word of the Lord. The priests and Levites consecrated themselves…and the Levites carried the ark of God with the poles on their shoulders" (vv.14, 15). They brought the ark into "the tent that David had pitched for it" with offerings, singing, and rejoicing. What a day! (16:1).

What did they learn through this experience? God didn't want new. He wanted obedience!

On an earlier occasion, Saul disobeyed the Lord's instructions after a battle. God said to destroy the Amalekites, including their king, and their plunder. Instead, he compromised and saved "the best of" the sheep and cattle to sacrifice to the Lord. Samuel's reply? "Does the Lord delight in burnt offerings and sacrifices as much as in obeying the voice of the Lord? To obey is better than sacrifice" (1 Samuel 22, 23).

Choose life in order that you may live
By loving the Lord your God,
By obeying His voice, and
By holding fast to Him.
—Deuteronomy 30:19–20

Three simple instructions:
Love the Lord!
Obey His voice!
Hold fast to Him!

Am I going to obey without question when God tells me to do something out of the ordinary? Three kings came to the prophet Elisha looking for help to beat the Moabites. The troops had been marching seven days and were exhausted. They were also out of water for themselves and their animals and could not continue. Out of respect for the king of Judah, Elisha was willing to go to God on their behalf. He asked for a harp and harpist, and through the beautiful music and the men's quietness, he heard the Lord say, "Tell them to make this valley full of ditches" (2 Kings 3:16). No problem! "This is an easy thing in the eyes of the Lord" (v.18). Start digging!

The next morning "about the time for offering the sacrifice, there it was—water flowing from the direction of Edom! And the land was filled with water" (2 Kings 3:20). The three kings won, the Moabites were wiped out, and God was glorified.

"Blessed are those who hear the Word
of God and obey it" (Luke 11:28).

PURSUE ME

A. Pursue (run after) righteousness.

"You, man of God (woman of God)…pursue *righteousness*, godliness, faith, love, endurance and gentleness" (1 Timothy 6:11). "The Lord rewards every man for his righteousness and faithfulness" (1 Samuel 26:23). "Abram believed the Lord, and He credited it to him as righteousness" (Genesis 15:6).

Right living, pleasing God in all we do, in the places we go, how we act toward others, what kind of example we are, the choices we make, the friends we pick—*this is pursuing righteousness* and is pursuing God, because God is righteous.

My hope is built on nothing less
Than Jesus' blood and righteousness.
I dare not trust the sweetest frame,
But wholly lean on Jesus' name.
—Edward Mote

Righteousness is as follows:

- ✓ Our GPS: "He leads me in paths of righteousness for His name's sake" (Psalm 23:3).
- ✓ Our food and drink: "Blessed are those who hunger and thirst for righteousness for they will be filled" (Matthew 5:6).
- ✓ Our treasure: "Seek first His kingdom and His righteousness, and all these things will be given to you as well" (Romans 5:18).
- ✓ Our clothing: "Stand firm then, with the belt of truth buckled around your waist..."
- ✓ Our protection: "With the breastplate of righteousness in place" (Ephesians 6:14).

B. Pursue (strive for) peace.

- ✓ Peace comes when I recognize that it's a blessing from God: "The Lord blesses His people with peace" (Psalm 29:11). "He will be called... Everlasting Father, Prince of Peace" (Isaiah 9:6).
- ✓ Peace comes when I let God rule my mind: "You will keep in perfect peace him whose mind is steadfast, because he trusts in you" (Isaiah 26:3). "The peace of God, which transcends all understanding, will guard your hearts and your minds in Christ Jesus" (Philippians 4:7).
- ✓ Peace comes when I let Christ rule my heart: "Let the peace of Christ rule in your hearts since as members of one body you were called to peace" (Colossians 3:15).

✓ Peace comes when I let God rule my body: "A heart at peace gives life to the body" (Psalm 119:30).

✓ Peace comes when I look for (ask for) it: "Seek peace and pursue it" (Psalm 34:14).

C. "Pursue...godliness..." (1 Timothy 6:11).

"Live peaceful and quiet lives in all *godliness* and holiness. This is good, and pleases God our Savior..." (1 Timothy 2:1–3). Does this mean the Christian who is striving to live a godly life will have it easy, that I will not suffer persecution? According to 2 Timothy 3:12, "Everyone who wants to live a godly life in Christ Jesus will be persecuted."

The *opposite of godliness* is godlessness, and Timothy writes, "Mark this: There will be terrible times in the last days" (2 Timothy 3:1). Here's a short list of what it will look like:

People will be lovers of themselves, lovers of money, disobedient, proud, abusive, ungrateful, unholy, unforgiving, without self-control, conceited, lovers of pleasure, and so on.

The godly man and woman will stand out like a sore thumb because we will be different. What does God's Word say to do?

Be a witness to others: "Don't be ashamed to testify about our Lord" (2 Timothy 1:8).

Be content: "Learn the secret of being content in every situation" (Philippians 4:11). "But *godliness* with contentment is great gain" (1 Timothy 6:6).

Be an encourager: "Encourage one another daily" (Hebrews 3:13).

Be a godly example: "Physical training is of some value, but *godliness* has value for all things, holding promise for both the present life and the life to come" (1 Timothy 4:8). "His divine power has given us everything we need for life and *godliness* through our knowledge of Him who called us by His own glory and goodness" (2 Peter 1:3).

Don't be satisfied with the status quo, but "Make every effort to add to your faith...perseverance; and to perseverance, *godliness*; and to *godliness*, brotherly kindness..." (2 Peter 1:5–7).

D.   "Pursue...gentleness..." (1 Timothy 6:11).

I think of a mother rocking her tiny babe to sleep. That is a picture of gentleness, but not the only one. The following verses from God's Word are the complete picture as God sees it. A godly man (or woman), using the full strength of his faith in the power of God, is one who controls his strength with meekness and gentleness. He or she is using strength under control. The person may be poised to erupt in anger but instead places himself under the Master's control, and the answer is gentle. The picture in my mind is one of a wild horse coming under the control of the rider. The horse is the same, with the same muscles, the same power, but the trainer has worked with it to bring that strength under the master's control with just a verbal command or slight pressure from the rider's leg.

"A *gentle* answer turns away wrath..." (Proverbs 15:1). "Always be prepared to give an answer to everyone who asks you to give the reason for the hope that you have. But do this with *gentleness* and respect" (1 Peter 3:15).

Am I gentle in my witness about Christ—my testimony? Do I place myself above the other person, looking down on them as somehow less than me? My prayer is that I will put on gentleness as clothing before I ever begin to share my faith. "Therefore, as God's chosen people, holy and dearly loved, clothe yourselves with compassion, kindness, humility, *gentleness* and patience" (Colossians 3:12).

"By the meekness and *gentleness* of Christ, I appeal to you" (2 Corinthians 10:1). "Let your *gentleness* be evident to all. The Lord is near" (Philippians 4:5). "But the fruit of the Spirit is love, joy, peace, patience, kindness, goodness, faithfulness, *gentleness* and self-control" (Galatians 5:22).

"I am *gentle* and humble in heart, and you will find rest for your souls" (Matthew 11:28). We come undemanding, clothed in humility, bowing before a holy God, remembering who He is.

E.   "Pursue...endurance..." (1 Timothy 6:11).

Definition for endurance: state or capability of lasting, even under pain or hardship; to remain firm under suffering.

Psalm 136 lists the psalmist's thanks to "the Lord," to the "God of gods," to the "Lord of lords," to the "God of heaven," enumerating God's goodness in creation, in His care for the nation Israel, right up to the current day, for "His love endures forever."

"You have been born again, not of perishable seed, but of imperishable, through the living and *enduring* word of God. For...the word of the Lord stands forever" (1 Peter 1:23, 25).

When my siblings and I were growing up and we had chores to do, there were times when we stopped to rest or picked up a book to look at. My mother, if she was working nearby, would say, with a grin, "Rest if you must, but don't quit." We knew it was something from her days of teaching in the one-room schoolhouse in Isanti County, Minnesota. There was a part of her that would always miss those days in the classroom, yet adamant that she gladly gave it up to bring up her children. This poem is not particularly Christian, but the premise is true. What the poem leaves out is the fact that I look to Jesus before everything else, not when everything else fails.

Don't Quit*

When things go wrong as
they sometimes will,
When the road you're trudging
seems all up hill,
When the funds are low
and the debts are high
And you want to smile,
but you have to sigh,
When care is pressing you down a bit,
Rest if you must, but don't you quit.

---

* Poem "Don't Quit" is in the public domain.

Life is strange with its twists and turns
As every one of us sometimes learns,
And many a failure comes about
When he might have won
had he stuck it out;
Don't give up though the
pace seems slow—
You may succeed with another blow.

Success is failure turned inside out—
The silver tint of the clouds of doubt,
And you never can tell just
how close you are,
It may be near when it seems so far;
So stick to the fight when
you're hardest hit—
It's when things seem worst
that you must not quit.
—John Greenleaf Whittier

"Everything that was written in the past was written to teach us, so that through *endurance* and the encouragement of the Scriptures we might have hope" (Romans 15:4).

How am I to gain these earmarks of a follower of Christ?

F. Read and memorize God's Word.

When Moses died, God spoke directly to Joshua and gave him His purpose—what God wanted him to do. "Do not let this Book of the Law depart from your mouth; meditate on it day and night, so that you may be careful to do everything written in it. Then you will be prosperous and successful" (Joshua 1:8).

Don't let My Word depart from your mouth. That was a bit confusing because it seemed as though when a person speaks the words are departing from the mouth. But it's just the opposite. When we talk about God's Word, it goes out from our mouth but only as a loud speaker or microphone would. Then we are to *meditate on it day and night* (in other words, think about it, Psalm 1:2 and 119:97) and *do everything written in it* (obey its commands fully, Ezra 7:10 and James 1:22–25). So talk about it! Obey it! And share with others! (Waalvoord and Zuck[*]).

When we know our purpose we can focus on it by listening to God's instructions and following His plan. God says to us, "Spend time with me. Read and study my Word." "Preserve sound judgment and discernment; do not let them out of your sight; they will be life for you" (Proverbs 3:21).

---

[*] The Bible Knowledge Commentary, Old Testament, based on the New International Version, 1985 SP Publications; Notes by John F. Walvoord and Roy B. Zuck, p. 329.

Early in our marriage Bob and I decided to memorize the book of James in the Phillips paraphrase. I typed up the chapters on index cards so he could have them in his truck and I could have a few in the kitchen. My intent was to work on memorizing while I went about doing chores. I got only one chapter put to memory, but, because the paraphrase is very easy to remember, even now, over forty years later, I can repeat the verses. There is nothing like repetition! A verse may not be easy to memorize, but if repeated every day for at least a week, it stays in the mind and heart for a very long time. "Oh how I love Your law! I meditate on it all day long" (Psalm 119:97).

Look at John 14:26 to see the value of memorizing Scripture: "The Counselor, the Holy Spirit, Whom the Father will send in My name, will teach you all things and will remind you of everything I have said to you." How can He remind us of something we have not hidden in our hearts? "I have hidden Your word in my heart that I might not sin against You" (Psalm 119:11).

Just as Jesus answered Satan in the wilderness temptation by using the Word from the book of Deuteronomy to refute Satan after each temptation, we also can use God's Word.

"So then we pursue the things which make for peace and the building up of one another" (Romans 14:19, Hebrews 12:14). "Seek peace and pursue it" (Psalm 34:14).

Memorizing is more difficult now but not impossible. I use as my example my mother, who, at age eighty, made her first overseas trip. This was a trip to Sweden that her four children gave her as a birthday gift. It just so happened that of the four siblings I was the most free to make the trip with her. It was a dubious honor because I could help zero with the language. But I trusted that the language her parents used in her childhood would come back from her memory when we needed it. And that was what happened.

In Sweden we visited Mom's cousins, the nieces and nephews her father left behind when he left for America in his late teens. He made the return trip once in his lifetime, when Mother was an infant and came back to Minnesota with his younger sister to help my grandmother care for the four older children.

That first night Mom and I were definitely not sleepy, with jet lag and excitement our main excuse! As we lay on the twin beds with the beautiful hand-cro-cheted-bordered sheets, we whispered and giggled softly, trying to wind down. I was not one to giggle with my mother, and maybe it was the jet lag, but it felt strangely comfortable, and giggle we did. After my dad died a few years earlier, Mother had been memorizing Scripture to help her get to sleep at night. She said now, "Do you want Colossians 3 or Psalm 91 or..." and she named some more chapters. I must say I was shocked.

If my children should ask me to recite a chapter or two on demand, could I do it? Actually I have been memorizing Scripture but definitely need to review more often. Since becoming a widow, I realize what a joy God's Word is in the "night watches."

"God my Maker, who gives songs in the night" (Job 35:10). "In His law he meditates day and night" (Psalm

1:2). "By day the Lord directs His love, at night His song is with me" (Psalm 42:8). "O satisfy us in the morning with Your loving-kindness, that we may sing for joy and be glad all our days" (Psalm 90:14).

G.   Memorize hymns and other Christian songs.

The old hymns of the church are like dessert to the soul that's weary and can't get to sleep. Why is it that I can recall the words to these songs, yet can't seem to keep the words to worship choruses longer than the morning service? Here's my very unscientific theory: the verses rhyme, the melody repeats, the chorus is consistent, and the meter is regular. But, for us seniors, the real reason is that they are familiar!

One of my dear aunts died a few years ago. Her husband, my mother's youngest brother, went regularly to visit her in the Alzheimer's unit where she was lovingly cared for when he no longer could. Every day he went in and helped her eat her meal, then sat down with her, and together they sang hymns from memory. Though other memories were gone, she knew all the words to these old favorites, which fed both their souls.

Songs (a line or phrase or entire song) and Bible verses learned as a child will be there when I need them most. God knows which words fit the need of my heart.

REMEMBER ME

Many of us have journals, diaries, scrapbooks, and photo albums to help us remember events or people or recipes or poetry or dates. In God's Word we read the different ways He instructed His people to remember Him and what they were taught:

In Numbers 15:37–40 the Lord gave instructions for a blue cord to be put on the tassels on the corners of their garments. This was so that they would always remember who they belonged to. "I am the Lord your God, who brought you out of Egypt to be your God. I am the Lord *your* God." You're mine!

In Deuteronomy 6 and 11 Moses instructs the Israelites to pass on to their children what God showed them through their forty years on the road. He charged the people: teach your children diligently...how to follow the Lord. Teach them on your walks while you do your chores together, when you go to bed at night, when you sit down to a meal. Tell them how much God loves them, how God kept them alive through that long journey, protecting them from the enemy, helping them to win battle after battle. Especially teach them about the Memorial Stones:

After Moses died, and Joshua became the leader of the vast company of the Israelites, God continued to give instructions about their welfare and their progress into the

Promised Land. They were to cross the Jordan River when it was at flood stage (Joshua 3:15). Then there came a test like they hadn't seen before. The previous generation (the parents of those crossing now) knew about this test of faith when they followed Moses across a dry ocean floor after the water split and piled up on each side. But this generation had to trust God for the same type of crossing.

With the Ark of the Covenant in view a great distance away, a path was made visible on a dry riverbed. Water piled upstream long enough for the entire population to cross to the other side. After all the people were safely across, the Lord told Joshua to have twelve men, one from each of the twelve tribes, to go back into the riverbed and each carry out one stone on their shoulder (so they must have been large). These were then carried to the place where the people were to lodge that night and later set up as an altar on Mount Ebal. (See Deuteronomy 27 and Joshua 8 for specific instructions.) Another twelve stones were placed in the center of the river where the priests stood with the Ark during the crossing. When the river returned to flood stage, these stones remained as visible reminders of God's love and care for His people.

"When your children ask...what are these stones? Then you shall tell them the Lord your God dried up the waters of the Jordan before you until you had crossed, just as the Lord your God had done to the Red Sea...that all the peoples of the earth may know that the hand of the Lord is mighty, so that you may fear the Lord your God forever" (Joshua 4:21–24).

"By this great miracle, the crossing of the Jordan River at flood stage by a nation of about 2 million people, God was glorified, Joshua was exalted, Israel was encouraged, and the Canaanites were terrorized" (Walvoord and Zuck*).

"*Remember* the former things, those of long ago; I am God, and there is no other; I am God, and there is none like Me" (Isaiah 46:8).

What about today? We don't have Joshua in front of the line showing us what to do…where to go…how to act. But we have God Himself ready at our call, willing to lead us in the way we should go. He is saying to us:
Remember Me…

- when I feel like I'm being tempted beyond what I am able to withstand.

---

* The Bible Knowledge Commentary, Old Testament, based on the New International Version, 1985 SP Publications; Notes by John F. Walvoord and Roy B. Zuck, p. 336.

"He will provide a way out so that you can stand up under it" (1 Corinthians 10:13).

- when the nights are long and morning seems very far away.

"My eyes stay open through the watches of the night, that I may meditate on Your promises" (Psalm 119:148).

- when I see the beauty of God's creation.

"Remember to extol His work" (Job 36:24).

- when I think about what Christ did for me on the cross (John 3:16).
- when I am filled with fear for the future.

"Remember this, fix it in mind... My purpose will stand, and I will do all that I please" (Isaiah 46:8, 11).

- when it doesn't seem as though my life is amounting to much.

"Find out what pleases the Lord" (Ephesians 5:1–20) by reading and studying His Word, and then obeying Him. Serve God's purpose, touch someone, make a difference. Spread the Good News about Jesus and His love.

"I am to be remembered from generation to generation" (Exodus 3:15).

I can fill my diary, my journal, with stories of my own experience as a follower of Christ. "Remember the wonders He has done, His miracles, and the judgments He pronounced (1 Chronicles 16:12).

Remember Me Today...

1. While I am young. "Remember your Creator in the days of your youth..." (Ecclesiastes 12:1).
2. God will help me to gain wisdom through His Word. "Teach us to number our days aright, that we may gain a heart of wisdom" (Psalm 90:12).
3. Use that wisdom to make decisions.
   - Be careful how I live.
   - Make the most of every opportunity.
   - Don't be foolish.
   - Understand what the Lord's will is (Ephesians 5:15–18).
4. Whether you turn to the right or to the left, your ears will hear a voice behind you, saying, "This is the way; walk in it" (Isaiah 30:21).

Lord Jesus, make Thyself to
me a living, bright reality,
More present to faith's vision keen
Than any outward object seen,
More dear, more intimately nigh
Than e'en the sweetest earthly tie.

—Unknown

SEEK ME

"God looks down from heaven on the sons of men to see if there are any who understand, any who *seek* God. Everyone has turned away, they have together become corrupt; there is no one who does good, not even one" (Psalm 53: 2, 3). My dear friends, this is why we need a Savior! "For God so loved the world that He gave His one and only Son, that whoever believes in Him shall not perish but have eternal life. For God did not send His Son into the world to condemn the world, but to save the world through Him" (John 3:16, 7).

One of the definitions for the word *pursue* is *seek*, and yet they are different. Pursue means to go after—the idea being chasing someone or something. One could *pursue* happiness, for instance. Go after it with all your might. Don't let it get away. While *seek* involves search, with the idea of looking for something until it is found, as "I won't stop searching for (*seeking*) my ring until I hold it in my hand."

Moses to the Israelites: "You are to *seek* the place the Lord your God will choose from among all your tribes to put His Name there for His dwelling" (Deuteronomy 12:5).

David to his son Solomon: "Acknowledge the God of your father, and serve Him with wholehearted devotion and with a willing mind, for the Lord searches every heart and understands every motive behind the thoughts. If you *seek* Him, He will be found by you; but if you forsake Him, He will reject you forever" (1 Chronicles 28:9).

The angel to the women at the tomb: "Why do you look for (*seek*) the living among the dead? He is not here; He has risen!" (Luke 24:5).

Jesus to Mary Magdalene: "Why are you crying? Who are you looking for (*seeking*)?" (John 20:15). Mary was crying so hard she couldn't see clearly, not even the One she was looking for. But when He called her name, she knew Him. Even so with me. I often look for Him and can't see Him for whatever is clouding my vision—worry, fear, sorrow, the business of the day. But then He calls me through the clouds, and I am freed to see Him.

God to us: "*Seek* the Lord while He may be found; call on Him while He is near" (Isaiah 55:6).

If you go to worship man-made gods and "if from there you *seek* the Lord your God, you will find Him if you look for Him with all your heart, and with all your soul" (Deuteronomy 4:29). "'I will be found by you,' declares the Lord, 'and will bring you back from captivity. I will gather you from all the nations and places where I have banished you,'" declares the Lord, "and will bring you back to the place from which I carried you into exile" (Jeremiah 29:14).

If people *seek* God, *seek* to walk in His ways, He promises to be found. He will never deliberately hide from His people. In John 1:1 Christ is called the Word. The Word was with God, and the Word was God. God is equal to the Word, Christ Jesus. In 2 Kings 22, Josiah, a godly king, was ruling his people to the best of his knowledge, doing what was right in the eyes of the Lord, and walking in all the ways of his ancestor David. But when Hilkiah, the High Priest, found the Book of the Law in the temple of the Lord and read the words to Josiah, the king tore his robes in grief. He had served God but did not know what God required until he read it in the Book. From that moment on he *sought* God wholeheartedly.

He went to the prophetess Huldah, who told the king what was required to follow the Lord completely. Following all the instructions he received, he removed all the gods, Asherah poles, altars to Baal, and destroyed everything that had to do with idol worship. The people celebrated the Passover to the Lord in Jerusalem for the first time "since the days of the judges who led Israel. Not throughout the days of the kings of Israel and the kings of Judah, had any such Passover been observed... Neither before nor after Josiah was there a king like him who turned to the Lord as he did—with all his heart and with all his soul and with all his strength" (2 Kings 22–25). Josiah sought the Lord, and the Lord heard him.

Seek God for Himself.
Seek not humility, seek God; then
humility will naturally come!

Seek not power, seek God; then
power will flow from you!
—Unknown

"If My people, who are called by My name, will humble themselves and pray and *seek* My face and turn from their wicked ways, then will I hear from heaven and will forgive their sin and will heal their land" (2 Chronicles 7:14).

"Ask and it will be given to you; *seek* and you will find; knock and the door will be opened to you. For everyone who asks receives; he who *seeks* finds; and to him who knocks, the door will be opened" (Matthew 7:7–8).

One day my three-year-old son came running through the house, calling, "Mommy, where are you?"

"Here I am in the dining room," I replied.

He ran in, saying happily, "Oh, hi, Mommy-in-the-dining-room!"

I suddenly thought about my prayers to the Father-which-art-in-heaven. I had assigned Him that place and had not given Him complete access to my heart, my home, and my life. He wants it all. He wants complete freedom to meet with me right where I am, all day and all night, lovingly caring for me and for my family: Heavenly Father, merciful Savior, indwelling Holy Spirit, prayer-answering God, friend of sinners. He's all that and more.

"'Am I only a God nearby,' declares the Lord, 'and not a God far away? Can anyone hide in secret places so that I cannot see him?' declares the Lord. 'Do not I fill heaven and earth?'" (Jeremiah 23:23, 24).

"Blessed are they who keep His statutes and *seek* Him with all their heart" (Psalm 119:2). "You will *seek* Me and find Me when you *seek* Me with all your heart. I will be found by you, declares the Lord" (Jeremiah 29:13).

"But *seek* first His kingdom and His righteousness, and all these things will be given to you as well" (Matthew 6:33). What things? Matthew writes about our need for food and drink, clothing, whatever causes us to lie awake worrying instead of sleeping. "In vain you rise early and stay up late, toiling for food to eat—for He grants sleep to those He loves" (Psalm 127:2).

My Heavenly Father knows that I need these things to sustain me and keep me going. It's just a matter of priority. If I seek Him first, He will provide everything that I need.

SERVE ME

What does the Lord need from me? A willing heart? Faithful service? A humble spirit? All of these.

In Mark 11:1–6 Jesus needed a donkey to ride into Jerusalem. He sent two of His disciples to the village with instructions for finding a colt tied there. It was just as He said, and they brought it to Jesus. Some neighbors questioned the disciples, but as soon as they said, "The Lord needs it" and promised to return it, "the people let them go."

In Luke 22:7–12 Jesus needed a room to celebrate the Passover. He sent two of His disciples, Peter and John, with instructions on how to find the place: "As you enter the city, a man carrying a jar of water will meet you. Follow him." What would be unusual about that? It was the women who fetched the water from the well. A man doing that chore would be easily recognizable. The disciples were to follow the man and to say to the owner of the house where he stopped, "The Teacher asks: 'Where is the guest room, where I may eat the Passover with My disciples?' He will show you a large upper room, all furnished. Make preparations there." They found things just as Jesus had told them.

What shall I give Thee, Master?
Thou who didst die for me,
Shall I give less of what I possess,
Or shall I give all to Thee?
Jesus, my Lord and Savior,
Thou hast giv'n all for me;
Thou didst leave Thy home above
To die on Calvary.
What shall I give Thee, Master?
Thou hast giv'n all for me;
Not just a part or half of my heart,
I will give all to Thee.
—Homer W. Grimes

"Be very careful to…love the Lord your God, to walk in all His ways, to obey His commands, to hold fast to Him and to *serve* Him with all your heart and all your soul" (Joshua 22:5). "It is the Lord your God you must follow, and Him you must revere… *Serve* Him and hold fast to Him" (Deuteronomy 13:4).

When our children were young, we camped by Jackson Lake Reservoir outside Truckee, California, with Grandma and Grandpa. The first night the kids enjoyed free rein on roasted marshmallows, eating as many as they wanted, so the next night the rule was *just two* for yourself and then as many as you want *for other people.* Their solution? "Nobody else wants one so I'm roasting one for him and he's roasting one for me." Serving each other with gladness!

When Joshua was nearing the end of his life, "He assembled all the tribes of Israel at Shechem. He summoned the elders, leaders, judges and officials of Israel, and they presented themselves before God" (Joshua 24:1). There was a special reason Joshua wanted them all to be there. It was to review the highlights of their journey to the Promised Land—how the Lord led them, cared for them, blessed them again and again.

I gave you a land on which you did not toil and cities you did not build; and you live in them and eat from vineyards and olive groves that you did not plant.

Now fear the Lord and *serve* Him with all faithfulness. Throw away the gods your forefathers worshiped beyond the River and in Egypt, and *serve* the Lord. But if *serving* the Lord seems undesirable to you, then choose for yourselves this day whom you will *serve,* whether the gods your forefathers served beyond the River, or the gods of the Amorites, in whose land you are living. But as for me and my household, we will *serve* the Lord. (Joshua 24:13–15)

After John the Baptist was born, his parents brought him to the synagogue to be circumcised on the eighth day. It was customary that he would also receive his name at that time. The neighbors and those present were about to name him Zechariah after his father, but Zechariah, who had been mute because of disbelief, wrote, "His name is John." Immediately, he began to speak and prophesied, "He has raised up a horn of salvation for us…to enable us to *serve Him* without fear in holiness and righteousness before Him all our days" (Luke 1:57–66).

Let me come closer to Thee, Jesus,
Oh, closer day by day;
Let me lean harder on Thee, Jesus,
Yes, harder all the way.

Let me show forth Thy beauty, Jesus,
Like sunshine on the hills;
Oh, let my lips pour forth Thy sweetness
In joyous, sparkling rills.

Yes, like a fountain, precious Jesus,
Make me and let me be;
Keep me, and use me daily, Jesus,

For Thee, for only Thee.

In all my heart and will, O Jesus,
Be altogether King;
Make me a loyal subject, Jesus,
To Thee in everything.

Thirsting and hungering for Thee, Jesus,
With blessed hunger here;
Longing for home on Zion's mountain,
No thirst, no hunger there.

—J. L. Lyne

It had been a very busy day off. Propped up in bed with my Bible and a cup of coffee, I began the day with a great quiet time and stayed where I was to write several cards. Laundry came next. After that I talked by phone to my daughter-in-law and grandson in Alaska for nearly an hour. Then I drove to DMV to renew my driver's license, started two chickens stewing, made four dozen muffins to take to missions potluck on Sunday, made three dozen cinnamon rolls, and finally sat down with Bob to a yummy-smelling pot roast dinner.

Throughout the day I sang with the radio, whistled, laughed, and had a great time; and all of a sudden I was exhausted. My attitude was rapidly sliding downhill in self-pity. Doesn't Bob recognize all my hard work? He could change everything by exclaiming with great fervor how delicious my dinner was. Lord, I need to hear it.

Bob might have wondered at the grin that came over my face just then, because in my heart I heard, "Well done, good and faithful servant." Yes, Bob said some nice things before the meal was over, but God knew I needed some encouragement at that moment before my sour attitude spoiled a perfectly good dinner. Service and sacrifice are a sweet-smelling offering to God and to those around us only if we surrender the need for recognition.

> For mercies so great, what
> return can I make
> For mercies so constant and sure;
> I'll love Him,
> I'll serve Him
> With all that I have
> As long as my life shall endure.
> —Thomas Chisholm

THANK ME

Luke 17 tells the story of ten lepers who were cleansed by Jesus:

Now on his way to Jerusalem, Jesus traveled along the border between Samaria and Galilee. As he was going into a village, ten men who had leprosy met him. They stood at a distance and called out in a loud voice, "Jesus, Master, have pity of us!" When He saw them, He said, "Go, show yourselves to the priests." And as they went, they were cleansed.

One of them, when he saw he was healed, came back, praising God in a loud voice. He threw himself at Jesus' feet and thanked Him—and he was a Samaritan. Jesus asked, "Were not all ten cleansed? Where are the other nine? Was no one found to return and give praise to God except this foreigner?"

Most children are taught to say "Thank you" almost as soon as they learn to talk. Why? Because it's a basic fundamental sign of gratitude, where he or she is not growing up expecting to be given whatever he wants—as entitlement. Where better to start learning to say "Thank you" than in the home with godly parents demonstrating with hearts full of thanksgiving, springing up in praise to God. The natural expression from a full heart.

My God
Today I kneel to say
"I thank You."
For once my prayer holds no request,
No names of friends for You to bless.
Because I think even You
Might sometimes like a prayer that's new;
Might like to hear somebody pray,
Who has no words but thanks to say.
Somebody satisfied and glad,
For all the joys that he has had,
And so I say again,
"I Thank You Lord."
—Unknown

Since moving to Alaska, my days have been filled with God's goodness. I have met several neighbors and found them warm and friendly. My kids and grandkids have been very thoughtful and loving, and I am always encouraged to let them know if I need anything, which I do. I have made many friends at church and am often invited out for lunch or coffee by one or two of these friendly seniors. I have grown accustomed to my electric stove and gas furnace and have a cozy warm home.

For several months, though, my heart was full of murmuring and complaining. I hate to admit it, but there was more than a trace of jealousy involved. Someone had a better view of the mountains. Someone else had a bigger house, a paved road, nicer landscaping, more garage storage, more windows to let in the winter light, and so on. It left me without joy by the end of the day. My selfish attitude was debilitating, and my time in the Word unproductive.

In reviewing Colossians 3, which I memorized a few years ago, I was brought up short by verse 15: "Let the peace of Christ rule in your heart…and be thankful." *Let* and *be* are passive words that must be allowed to penetrate the heart, or they are not worth anything. God made that verse come alive in my heart, and I began to thank Him for what He has done for me, given me.

Because He led me to this house, I thanked Him for it. Because my house is on this street I thanked Him for it. Because I can see the tops of some mountains, I thanked Him for the view. Because my street gets plowed on heavy snow days, I thanked Him that I live within city limits. Because my neighbors are kind, I thanked Him for them.

As God's children we are commanded to give thanks in *everything*. In *every* situation there is *always* something for which we can be thankful. Many of the Psalms, and especially Psalm 136, are full of the reminder to "give thanks to the Lord, for He is good. His love endures forever," ending with v. 26, "Give thanks to the God of heaven. His love endures forever."

"Give thanks in *all* circumstances, for *this* is God's will for you in Christ Jesus" (1 Thessalonians 5:18).

This circumstance,
This situation,
This coworker,
This family member,
This setback…

is God's will. He allowed it. Don't fight it. It is for your highest good. "In *all* things God works for the good of those who love Him" (Romans 8:28). What is our ultimate good? "That we would be conformed to the likeness of His Son" (v. 29). Why is it so important to give thanks in everything? That we might be like Jesus!

Thank you, Lord,
for the peace,
the joy,
the adventure,

that commitment to you really brings.
—Pastor Bruce Heiple[*]

What a privilege to spend many years in Minnesota among my Swedish family—grandparents, aunts, uncles, cousins—most of whom were singers! I still remember a few lines of "He the Pearly Gates Will Open" in Swedish, and this song of thanksgiving sung by two aunts:

Thanks to God for my Redeemer, Thanks
for all Thou dost provide!
Thanks for times now but a memory,
Thanks for Jesus by my side!
Thanks for pleasant, balmy springtime,
thanks for dark and dreary fall!
Thanks for tears by now forgotten, Thanks
for peace within my soul!

Thanks for prayers that Thou hast
answered, thanks for what Thou dost
deny!
Thanks for storms that I have weathered,
thanks for all Thou dost supply!

---

[*] Quote by Dr. Bruce Heiple, pastor Sierra Presbyterian Church, Nevada City California from 1992–2002. Used by permission.

Thanks for pain and thanks for pleasure,
    thanks for comfort in despair!
Thanks for grace that none can measure,
    thanks for love beyond compare!

Thanks for roses by the wayside, Thanks
    for thorns their stems contain!
Thanks for home and thanks for fireside,
Thanks for hope, that sweet refrain!
Thanks for joy and thanks for sorrow,
    Thanks for heav'nly peace with Thee!
Thanks for hope in the tomorrow, Thanks
    thru all eternity!
        —August Ludwig Storm (trans-
        lated by Carl E. Backstrom)

"We give thanks to you, O God; we give thanks, for your Name is near" (Psalm 75:1).

Praise to the Lord, the Almighty,
    the King of creation!
Oh my soul, praise Him, for He
    is thy health and salvation!
All you who hear, now to
His temple draw near;
Join me in glad adoration!

Praise to the Lord, who o'er all
things so wondrously reigneth,

Shelters thee under His wings,
yea, so gently sustaineth!
Hast thou not seen how all
thy longings have been
Granted in what He ordaineth?

Praise to the Lord! O let all
that is in me adore Him!
All that hath life and breath, come
now with praises before Him.
Let the Amen sound from
His people again;
Gladly for aye we adore Him.

—Joachim Neander
(translated by Catherine Winkworth)

Songs of praise, springing from the depth of emotion
and beautiful words, to simple words, expressing the need
of the heart and soul to be thankful!

Thank you, Lord, for saving my soul;
Thank you, Lord, for making me whole;
Thank you, Lord, for giving to me

Thy great salvation so rich and free.
        —Seth and Bessie Sykes

"Let everything that has breath praise
the Lord (give thanks)" (Psalm 150:6).

In the verbs below you (or I) are the subject, though not stated specifically. So you and I are the ones doing the action. We do what is necessary in the light of Scripture in order to fulfill God's direction, or purpose, at the time. It's a choice, but God's Word makes it clear that in order to do what's pleasing to Him we follow Him, and do what He asks.

Colossians 3:13–16:

Be thankful
Put on love
Bear with each other
Do all in the name of the Lord Jesus
Forgive as the Lord forgave you.
Give thanks to God the Father
Sing with gratitude in your hearts
Let the peace of Christ rule…
Let the word of Christ dwell…

"Speak to one another with psalms, hymns and spiritual songs. Sing and make music in your heart to the Lord, always giving thanks to God the Father for everything in the name of our Lord Jesus Christ" (Ephesians 5:19, 20). "From the fullness of His grace we have all received one blessing after another" (John 1:16). "Why are you downcast O my soul? Why so disturbed within me? Put your hope in God, for I will yet praise Him, my Savior and my God" (Psalm 42:11).

In the depths of my life, at the root of my coming together with other believers, is a precious ministry called fellowship. Fellowship with men and women and fellowship with God. All are important in my life. Loneliness, or living a life completely alone, without friends, is not God's plan. Fellowship is one of the choices I can make in order to live a fuller life—a life of increased possibilities for friendship and reaching out to others who might need my touch, my brand of hope and mercy.

"God, who has called you into fellowship with His Son Jesus Christ our Lord, is faithful" (1 Corinthians 1:9). "Our fellowship is with the Father and with His Son, Jesus Christ... If we claim to have fellowship with Him yet walk in the darkness, we lie and do not live by the truth. But if we walk in the light, as He is in the light, we have fellowship with one another, and the blood of Jesus, His Son, purifies us from all sin" (1 John 1:3, 7).

How awesome of God to have the idea for the perfect companion of the man He created. A wife! It can be, and should be, the sweetest relationship ever. Especially exciting is the fact that God said, "It's good" to all the things He created; but when man was wandering around the Garden of Eden by himself, God said, "This is not good! He needs a helper suitable for him!"

"Now the Lord God had formed out of the ground all the beasts of the field and all the birds of the air. He brought them to the man to see what he would name them; and whatever the man called each living creature that was its name. So the man gave names to all the livestock, the birds of the air and all the beasts of the field.

"But for Adam no suitable helper was found. So the Lord God caused the man to fall into a deep sleep; and while he was sleeping, He took one of the man's ribs and closed up the pace with flesh. Then the Lord God made a woman from the rib He had taken out of the man, and He brought her to the man" (Genesis 2:18-22). Imagine what that might have been like! The woman was God's wise answer to man's need for a suitable helper.

When my husband died, I realized the emptiness in many ways. My life was no longer *us two*, but *me alone*. If I was the answer to Bob's need for a suitable helper, I needed to fill the loss with others who might need what I could offer—friendship, first of all.

In the process of time I began to introduce myself to women who looked close to my age (or younger, as I became better acquainted) and began accepting invitations to lunch once or twice a week. Before long I was doing the inviting to my home or to a coffee shop in town.

One restaurant became my favorite go-to place for coffee and pie or a meal. I found it easier to share verbally with one woman at a time and to encourage that woman in her walk with the Lord. I am sometimes teased about renting a booth in this restaurant as my *office*. If it's my choice where to meet a friend, I nearly always choose this place in the middle of town that has been here nearly since the town began! It is cozy and comfortable, and the view on a clear day is breathtaking. The snow-covered mountain directly opposite is featured on many brochures and calendars from the area. It also is a place full of memories, as a place where Bob and I often went for coffee on visits to our Alaska family.

With the repeated visits, either alone or with a friend, I began learning the servers by name. It gave me a chance to ask questions, listen, seek to befriend them, and share God's love.

TRUST ME

"The Lord has made everything for His own purpose" (Proverbs 16:4). Not mine. His. I can trust Him…with all my heart. I can stop leaning on my own unstable understanding (perception) of the situation, start acknowledging (recognizing) Him as Lord, and watch as He directs my paths according to *His* purpose, *His* plan (Proverbs 3:5, 6). "It is God Who works in you to will and to act according to *His* good purpose" (Philippians 2:13).

Tis so sweet to trust in Jesus, just to take
    Him at His word,
Just to rest upon His promise, just to
    know, "Thus saith the Lord."
Jesus, Jesus, how I trust Him! How I've
    proved Him o'er and o'er!
Jesus, Jesus, precious Jesus! O for grace to
    trust Him more!
           —Louisa M. R. Stead

According to my understanding of the situation, a dear one was making a bad choice, and my heart was breaking. I had much turmoil as to what to say or do. Knowing it wasn't my place to say or do anything, I committed it to the Lord. The words came into my mind, "Trust in the Lord with all your heart, and lean not on your own understanding." Pastor Greg Kuehn, my pastor in Reno, had just preached a sermon in which he talked about the "understanding" as being "your own perception of the situation." A huge peace followed.

Weeks later, more words came: "You will know the truth and the truth will set you free." Along with it came the mental picture of these dear ones I had been praying for. I knew it had something to do with them. Later that same day a phone call came from them with news that clarified everything and brought tears of joy and thanksgiving.

Oh, how sweet to trust in Jesus! I've proved over and over that this One I am trusting with my life is faithful. I can take Him at His word. He will never fail. Trust is based on knowledge; and this knowledge is gained by spending time together, reading His Word, talking together as friend to friend, father to child. As a child of God I take one small leap at a time into my Father's arms, and trust begins to build.

It has been the hardest for me to trust when...

a. my music was leaving, drifting away,
b. my days and nights seemed to go on forever,
c. the loneliness was pressing me down,
d. I felt misunderstood, and
e. it seemed God was not answering my prayer.

Oh, for grace to trust Him more!

In 1 Samuel 29 and 30 is the story of David's escape to the land of the Philistines, where he put himself under the protection of Achish, king of Gath, and settled there with his family. When Achish went to war with the Israelites, David was tremendously disappointed to be sent home after the elders expressed distrust over his loyalty. But he went, along with his six hundred men. He arrived home to find that his two wives, and all the families of his men, had been taken captive.

With God's help, he was able to chase after the Philistines and get back their families along with great amounts of plunder. What would have happened if he had been allowed to fight with Achish? We don't know. But because he didn't balk at the order, God took his disappointment and used it as His appointment to save his people.

Can I face crushing disappointment as His appointment, whether or not I ever know the reason? It's what is called *trust*.

"Commit your way to the Lord, *trust* also in Him, and He will do it" (Psalm 37:5). "*Trust* in the Lord with all your heart and do not lean on your own understanding" (Proverbs 3:5).

The question isn't "What if?" but "What is?"

"What if" pursues the negative. "What is" claims the positive. What is the truth?

The Israelites were caught in a war against their enemies in 1 Chronicles 5, but "God handed the Hagrites and all their allies over to them, because they cried out to Him during the battle. He answered their prayers, because they trusted in Him."

How good is the God we adore,
Our faithful unchangeable Friend!
His love is as great as His power,
And knows neither measure nor end!

'Tis Jesus the First and the Last,
Whose Spirit shall Guide us safe home
We'll praise Him for all that is past,
And trust Him for all that's to come.
                              —Joseph Hart

"You will keep in perfect peace him whose mind is steadfast, because he *trusts* in You. *Trust* in the Lord forever, for the Lord, the Lord, is the Rock eternal" (Isaiah 26:3–4).

When Bob and I moved to a small town in the foothills of the Sierra Nevada Mountains, we did so to get out of big city life, along with big city traffic, and to return to a special place Bob loved as a child. He took a job teaching in a

Christian middle and high school at two-thirds cut in pay, trusting God to supply our needs. He did. One blessing after another. To begin with (a) our children were allowed to attend tuition-free. (b) Besides this, we were given anonymous money gifts and food boxes, money for new tires, interest-free loans...and we made it through the first year.

When it came time to sign the contract for the second year, we had a slight hesitation, but signing seemed the right thing to do. Third year? The Christian school needed a signed contract in May, while the public schools didn't hire until August. We prayed for wisdom and were both sure that God was directing us to give notice. He would not be going back to that teaching position.

Bob applied to the public junior high in town for a counseling job, being quite sure it would be his. The interview came and went, and we waited at home, not wanting to leave the house for fear we'd miss the phone call.

All things humanly speaking pointed toward his appointment. Bob had seventeen years of experience in junior high schools, and we believed it was for him. We trusted in God's promise that when we step out in faith, He leads us in the way we should go and He honors that faith.

It was not to be. We got the letter stating Bob was not chosen, and we were shocked. I was very shaken. "Lord, you said that without faith it is impossible to please you. We have faith. We believe. Are you not pleased?" God's answer was, "I like your faith. It pleases me. It's just not what I have in mind."

To show us that our God was able to supply all of our needs and could be trusted beyond any ability or back-up plan of ours, we were handed a "payment due" bill for $2,000 for capital gains tax, which cleared out our savings.

After three more years of seeing our needs supplied miracle after miracle and applying for job after job to no avail, we were ready. A full-time job opened up in another state. Bob applied, had an interview five days later, and was hired the next day. We moved across the border to Nevada and spent the next twenty-five years telling everyone our story. God is faithful!

In a nutshell: "When he falls, he will not be hurled headlong, because the Lord is the One who holds his hand" (Psalm 37:24).

"*Grow* in the grace and knowledge of our Lord and Savior Jesus Christ" (2 Peter 3:18). Growing is a process. It does not come at once. A baby is carried everywhere at first. In the process of time, he pulls himself up to a standing position and finally takes a small wobbling step. These steps become more sure and steady, and the baby moves on through the stages: young child, older child, and, finally, adulthood.

When our son graduated from UNR, the verse on his graduation announcement said, "For I know the plans I have for you, says the Lord. Plans to prosper you and not to harm you. Plans to give you hope and a future" (Jeremiah 29:11). My prayer was, *Lord, this son is Yours and has been since he was an infant. Use Him for Your own purpose. Prosper him as he trusts in You.*

"I eagerly expect and hope that I will in no way be ashamed, but will have sufficient courage so that now as always Christ will be exalted (magnified, brought near as with a telescope) in my body, whether by life or by death"(Philippians 1:20). Note: Descriptive words within the parentheses are un-named in my notebook from years past.

"I trust in Your unfailing love; my heart rejoices in Your salvation. I will sing to the Lord, for He has been good to me" (Psalm 13:5–6).

Importance of Friends

In the book of Ezra, the exiles had been unfaithful to God. Ezra prostrated himself praying, weeping, and confessing before the house of God. In answer to prayer, a very large assembly gathered to him from Israel, the people weeping bitterly and confessing their unfaithfulness. Ezra's friend Shecaniah supported his desire to promote the law of God and said to him, "Do what you need to do. We will support you, so take courage and do it." Shecaniah was a faithful friend and encourager, saying, "There is hope for Israel in spite of this" (Ezra 10:4).

In Exodus 17, Joshua, at Moses's command, began to fight against Amalek. Moses promised to stand on the top of the hill with the staff of God in his hand, so Aaron and Hur, not wanting to leave him alone, went up with him. When Moses held his hands up, Israel prevailed, and when he let his hands down, Amalek prevailed. But Moses's hands grew heavy. So his friends put their heads together to find a solution. They brought a large stone for him to sit on, and Aaron and Hur stood one on each side of their friend and supported his hands. In this way his hands were steady until the sun set, and Joshua overwhelmed the Amalekites.

When do you and I need courage? Perhaps one of these is a weak spot?

1. Courage to face the day—give God your schedule.
2. Courage to face the night—commit it to God, memorize His Word and use it to face the darkness.
3. Courage to face the future—God will be with me even when I am dying. "Even though I walk through the valley of the shadow of death (valley of deep darkness) I fear no evil, for You are with me" (Psalm 23:4).
4. Courage to face the mirror—make friends with the man/woman in the mirror "that you may please Him in every way, growing in the knowledge of God" (Colossians 1:10).

I believe God has a wonderful sense of humor to help us through times like this. Just look at 2 Corinthians 4:16 and 18, "We do not lose heart. Though outwardly we are wasting away, yet inwardly we are being renewed day by day… So we fix our eyes not on what is seen, but on what is unseen. For what is seen is temporary, but what is unseen is eternal."

When we receive our transformed body on the way up to heaven, there will be no more wrinkles, age spots, or bags under the eyes. Hallelujah!

Courage is tied in with faith and love, and we can hardly have one without the others. Read what Paul says in his letter to the church at Thessalonica:

"Your *faith is growing* more and more, and the love every one of you has for each other is increasing" (2 Thessalonians 1:3).

Look at Matthew 14:27 and Mark 6:50: In the fourth watch of the night He (Jesus) came to them, walking on the sea. When the disciples saw Him walking on the sea, they were terrified and said, *It is a ghost!* And they cried out in fear. But immediately Jesus spoke to them, saying, "*Take courage. It's Me! Don't be afraid."* What an incredible reminder of who we are, who I am, a child of God. What dad would let his child be terrified of their own father? *Hey! It's me! Daddy!*

I must grow in the knowledge of the Lord Jesus so I will know who is on my side and…know my enemy, from Ephesians 6:

- The rulers of this dark world
- The authorities of this dark world

- The powers of this dark world
- Spiritual forces of evil in the heavenly realms

Before I ever leave my room in the morning, my instruction is get dressed! From Colossians 3 and Ephesians 6

1. *Put on* the Lord Jesus Christ.
2. *Take off* your old self.
3. *Put on* the new self.
4. *Clothe yourself* with compassion, kindness, humility, gentleness and patience.
5. *Put on* love, which binds them all together in perfect unity.
6. *Put on* the whole armor of God.
7. *Stand* your ground.
8. *Put on* the armor of light (Romans 13:12).

> Moses said to the people, "Do not fear! Stand by and see the salvation of the Lord which He will accomplish for you today... The Lord will fight for you while you keep silent" (Exodus 14:13, 14, NASB).

Required garments:

a. Belt of *truth* buckled around my waist
b. Breastplate of *righteousness* in place
c. Feet fitted with the readiness that comes from the gospel of *peace*

  d. The shield of *faith*, with which I can extinguish all the flaming arrows of the evil one

  e. The helmet of *salvation*

  f. The sword of the Spirit, which is the *Word of God*

9. Pray.

  In the spirit
  On *all* occasions
  With *all* kinds of prayers and requests

10. *Be on the alert.*

11. *Always keep on* praying for *all* the saints.

I will praise the Lord, Who counsels me;
even at night my heart instructs me.

I have set the Lord always before me.
Because He is at my right
hand, I will not be shaken.
Therefore my heart is glad
and my tongue rejoices;

My body also will rest secure,
because You will not abandon
me to the grave,
nor will You let Your Holy One see decay.

You have made known to
me the path of life;
You will fill me with joy in Your presence,
with eternal pleasures at Your right hand.
—Psalm 16:7–11

WATCH FOR ME

When my children were young, we attended a neighborhood Bible class together. The children had the same lessons as the moms, greatly simplified in presentation but not in content. We must have been studying Christ's being taken up to heaven after the resurrection, because that was where the conversation was going on our walk home. I was busy with my thoughts when I noticed my kids had stopped walking and were holding up cardboard craft projects just made in class—two small cardboard rolls held together with tape. I watched for a minute as they looked up into the sky through their "binoculars."

"What are you doing?"

"Looking for Jesus!"

Just like my children, "The disciples were looking intently up into the sky as (Jesus) was going, when two men dressed in white stood beside them... *This same Jesus*" is coming back! (Acts 1:10–11). "No one knows about that day or hour, not even the angels in heaven, nor the Son, but *only the Father!* Therefore, keep watch because you do not know on what day your Lord will come" (Matthew 24:36, 42).

God keeps His promises. That we know for sure. So "Be on guard! Be alert! You do not know when that time will come... Therefore keep watch... What I say to you, I say to everyone: Watch!" (Mark 13:33–37).

What to do until Jesus calls us Home:

1. Hold unswervingly to the hope we profess (Hebrews 10:23).
2. Spur one another on toward love and good deeds (v. 24).
3. Don't give up meeting together (v. 25).
4. Encourage one another—and all the more as we see the Day approaching (v. 25).

We need each other!

Paul wrote in his letter to the Thessalonians that we should encourage each other with God's Word about the second coming of Christ, and the joy of one day being with Him in glory! (1 Thessalonians 4:17). Also, he says, "Encourage the timid, help the weak, be patient with everyone...be kind, be joyful always; pray continually; give thanks in all circumstances, for this is God's will for you in Christ Jesus (5:14–16).

I believe God is pleased and glorified when we live out our walk and relationship to Jesus in this way.

5. Don't neglect Holy Communion—"For whenever you eat this bread and drink this cup, you proclaim the Lord's death until He comes" (1 Corinthians 11:26).
6. Fight the good fight (2 Timothy 4:7).
7. Finish the race (v. 7).
8. Keep the faith (v. 7).
9. Expect persecution (2 Timothy 3:12).
10. "Forgive each other, just as in Christ God forgave you" (Ephesians 4:32).
11. Take captive every thought to make it obedient to Christ (2 Corinthians 10:5).
12. Make every effort to be found spotless, blameless, and at peace with Him (2 Peter 3:14).
13. Always give myself fully to the work of the Lord (1 Corinthians 15:58).
14. If it is possible, as far as it depends on me, I should live at peace with everyone (Romans 12:18).

To live above with friends you love,
Oh, that will be glory.
But to live below with friends you know,
Well, that's another story!
—Unknown

More instructions for the rest of my life:

> Be on your guard;
> stand firm in the faith;
> be men (women) of courage;
> be strong.
> Do everything in love.
> —1 Corinthians 16:13

Praying for my children, grandchildren, and now great-grandchildren has always been a privilege, and a charge from God. As I wait for, and watch for, the return of Christ, I have the joy of reinforcing their parents' lessons and instruction by my choice of books, movies, friendships, behavior, conversation, and anything else that could show what I believe and Who I worship and follow.

In 2 Timothy 4:2, the apostle Paul gave specific instructions to the young pastor, Timothy: "Preach the Word; be prepared in season and out of season (when it's convenient and when it isn't); encourage—with great patience and careful instruction."

These verses are true for anyone who has contact with children. "Fix these words of mine in your hearts and minds… Teach them…talking about them when you sit at home and when you walk along the road, when you lie down and when you get up" (Deuteronomy 11:18, 19).

What I must be constantly aware of in working with little ones:

Don't preach *at* them.
Live godly *before* them.
Demonstrate Love *to* them.
Model Christ *for* them.
Ask forgiveness *of* them.

The greatest privilege to be granted a grandparent is to get a phone call from a grandchild with the precious voice saying, "Memaw (Mamaw or Gramma, I am called all three), I asked Jesus in my heart!" There is no greater joy!

"The Lord Himself will come *down* from heaven… and the dead in Christ will rise first. After that, we who are still alive…will be caught *up*." We'll meet *in the air* and will be with the Lord forever.

"Therefore encourage each other with these words" (1 Thessalonians. 4:16–18).

"But as for me, I watch in hope for the Lord, I wait for God my Savior" (Micah 7:7).

"He who testifies to these things says, 'Yes, I am coming soon.' Amen. Even so come, Lord Jesus" (Revelation 22:20).

"Listen, I tell you a mystery: We will not all sleep, but we will all be changed—in a flash, *in the twinkling of an eye*, at the last trumpet. For the trumpet will sound, the dead will be raised imperishable, and we will be changed" (1 Corinthians 15:51, 52).

Bob and I knew without any doubt that all four of our parents were ready to meet God when He called them home. Bob's mom walked out the back door to hang some things on the clothesline, and stepped instead into heaven. That was hard for the family, but a wonderful "step" for her.

My father-in-law lived with us for a time after his wife died. He was confused and lonely and wanted only to go home. With each new day the questions were the same. "Mom died, didn't she? When was that? Where were we living when she died? How did I get here? Did Mom make these plans for me before she died? How long have I been here?" The family knew he couldn't live alone. Mother was his constant companion, his rock and safe place.

As the days lengthened and the sun grew warm, Dad spent hours sitting on the patio, looking and listening, waiting. One day I saw him look up suddenly and begin to mouth words, his arm outstretched to someone unseen. "Mom was here. She talked to me." Two months later he went to be with her and with his Lord. What I remember best about his final months was his mealtime prayer, which nearly always included the phrase, "That we might be a witness to others of your love and grace and saving power." Dad was ready to go!

My parents celebrated their golden wedding anniversary a few weeks before Dad died at age seventy-five. For years Dad would find the quiet of a basement room in their home in the night hours a solace and a haven for meeting with His Lord. His favorite song was realized during these basement hours.

He giveth more grace when
the burdens grow greater;
He sendeth more strength
when the labors increase;
To added affliction He addeth His mercy,
To multiplied trials, His multiplied peace.
His love has no limit, His
grace has no measure;
His pow'r has no boundary
known unto men;
For out of His infinite riches in Jesus
He giveth and giveth and giveth again.
　　　　　　　　—Don Moen

After he was gone Mother lived another twenty years in good health and died at ninety-five. God was gracious and gave her what she asked for, a clear mind to pray daily through her lengthy prayer list and a sharp mind to work crossword puzzles and to enjoy a competitive game of Scrabble. Before she died, Mom talked about this prayer list. "Who is going to pray for all these people?" When I assured her that her family would continue taking her requests to the Lord, she replied with a spark in her eyes, "It's not easy! It's hard!"

Here is His Word to you and me: "'*My grace* is sufficient for you, for *My power* is made perfect in weakness.' Therefore I will boast all the more gladly about my weaknesses, so that Christ's power may rest on me. That is why, for Christ's sake, I delight in weaknesses… For when I am weak, then I am strong" (2 Corinthians 12: 9, 10). And more: "In quietness and trust is your strength" (Isaiah 30:15). Christ is all I need for the days ahead. I can trust Him and tell others of His goodness and mercy.

Say, will you be ready when Jesus comes?
Are you truly born again,
washed in Jesus' blood?
Are your garments spotless—
are they white as snow?
Will you be ready when Jesus comes?

Two shall be together
grinding at the mill,
Two will be together
sleeping calm and still.

One shall be taken, and
the other left behind;
Will you be ready when Jesus comes?
—Author Unknown
(Sung in my childhood in the 1940's in Minnesota)

Perfect submission, all is at rest.
I in my Savior am happy and blest;
Watching and waiting, looking above,
Filled with His goodness, lost in His love.
—Fanny J. Crosby

WORSHIP ME

"Come, let us worship and bow down. Let us kneel before the Lord our Maker, for He is our God, and we are the people of His pasture and the sheep of His hand" (Psalm 95:6, 7). "For from Him and through Him and to Him are all things. To Him be the glory forever" (Romans 11:36).

Worship Me—with my life, my conversation, my thoughts. I must stop mulling over and meditating on all my failures of yesterday or last week or even that event years ago when I felt like a complete failure. How can I come to a Holy God with my past? I can, because of who God is, not who I am. He says "Come" and when I don't, I call Him a liar, incapable, unwilling, and weak.

"The Love of Christ...surpasses knowledge" (Ephesians 3:19).

"The peace of God...surpasses comprehension" (Philippians. 4:7).

"The power of God...surpasses greatness" (2 Corinthians 4:7).

Worship Him!

In Revelation 5, John saw "a mighty angel proclaiming in a loud voice, 'Who is worthy to break the seals and open the scroll?' But no one in heaven or on earth or under the earth could open the scroll or even look inside it. (John) wept and wept because no one was found worthy." But One *was* found worthy! Jesus, "the Lion of the tribe of Judah, the Root of David," is able to open the scroll.

"You are worthy, our Lord and God, to receive glory and honor and power, for You created all things, and by Your will they were created and have their being" (Revelation 4:11).

After John saw all that the angel showed him, he immediately fell down to worship at the feet of the angel. "But he said to me, 'Do not do it! I am a fellow servant with you and with your brothers the prophets and of all who keep the words of this book. Worship God!'" (Revelation 2:8, 9).

All through the Bible, Old Testament and New Testament, I see reference after reference where someone comes into contact with the Holy God and is moved to fall to the ground in worship. Over and over God gives His Name. I Am! All things, everything, all I need, my constant help in trouble, my Shepherd, my Bread, my shelter, my Life. He alone was found worthy.

Ascribe to the Lord, O mighty ones,
Ascribe to the Lord glory and strength.

Ascribe to the Lord the
glory due His name;
Worship the Lord in the
splendor of His holiness.
　　　　　　　—Psalm 29:1–2

Taking God's Name in vain is so common in our culture that we don't even *hear* it anymore. Many are so accustomed to the use of "God" or "Lord," and even "Jesus Christ" in everyday conversation, that the words have lost their meaning. Children hear it from adults and understand that it's okay. To stop a child and call attention to what they just said just bewilders them. What's wrong with it? Everybody does it!

But from Genesis to Revelation when one is struck with the necessity to worship, he immediately falls on his face as though unable to remain standing. His Name alone is powerful enough (Proverbs 18:10). "The Name of the Lord is a strong (fortified) tower. The righteous run to it and are safe."

In the Exodus story of Moses leading the children of Israel through the wilderness, God had to continually remind the people, His people, who He was. They forgot from one major exhibition of His power to another, maybe the very next day, that He is holy, to be worshipped. In return for these miracles of His grace, the people complained, grumbled, threatened to go back to Egypt, disobeyed, brought dishonor to His Name (Num. 20:13).

"The Lord your God is God of gods and Lord of lords, the great God, mighty and awesome… Fear the Lord your God and serve Him. Hold fast to Him… He is your praise; He is your God, Who performed for you those great and awesome wonders you saw with your own eyes" (Deuteronomy 10:17, 20–21).

In speaking to the Israelites just before he was to die, Moses gave a powerful message in the form of a song (Deuteronomy 32:1–43). At the end he said to them, "Take to heart all the words I have solemnly declared to you this day, so that you may command your children to obey carefully all the words of this law. They are not just idle words for you—they are your life" (vv. 46, 47).

"Exalt the Lord our God and worship at His footstool; He is holy" (Psalm 99:5). "It is God's will that you should be holy" (1 Thessalonians. 4:3). "You are worthy, our Lord and God, to receive glory and honor and power, for You created all things, and by Your will they were created and have their being" (Revelation 4:11). "Holy, holy, holy is the Lord Almighty; the whole earth is full of His glory" (Isaiah 6:3).

"O Lord, our Lord, how majestic is Your name in all the earth! You have set Your glory above the heavens. From the lips of children and infants You have ordained praise because of Your enemies, to silence the foe and the avenger" (Psalm 8:1, 2).

When God had a message for the people of Israel and asked who was available to deliver it, Isaiah answered, "Here I am. Send me!" before he knew what God wanted. He was struck by the holiness of the Lord and feared that he would die, so he would have done anything. "My eyes have seen the King, the Lord Almighty" (Isaiah 6:5).

In a vision, Isaiah saw the Lord "high and lifted up, and the train of His robe filled the temple. Seraphs were calling to each other as they flew: 'Holy, holy, holy is the Lord Almighty; the whole earth is full of His glory... At the sound of their voices the doorposts and thresholds shook and the temple was filled with smoke" (Isaiah 6:1, 3–4). Praise and glory to the Lord God Most High!

The message Isaiah was called to carry was one of sorrow and sadness for the children of Israel. But he also carried a prophetic new message to Ahaz—a sign from the Lord Himself: "The virgin will be with child and will give birth to a son, and will call Him Immanuel."

I am overwhelmed at what I find in 1 Samuel, chapter 1: Hannah, being barren all her married life and constantly ridiculed by Elkanah's other wife, earnestly prayed year after year for a child. This promised child was to be given to the service of the Lord. God answered her prayer with a beloved son whom she named Samuel. When he was weaned, she brought him to the house of the Lord at Shiloh just as she promised Eli. "*And he worshiped the Lord there*" (1 Samuel 1:28). From birth Hannah taught him to love and worship the Lord God. What a testimony to his parents' own heart of worship that he should follow their example when on his own.

"From the lips of children and infants you have ordained praise" (Psalm 8:3).

One Sunday morning something happened in the worship service that illustrates this verse so well. The toddler couldn't have been more than eighteen months old. He loved going to church. He loved to sing. It showed in his eyes, on his face, as soon as the music started. Often, while we stood to sing, his daddy held him up in his arms or helped him stand on the back of the forward pew so he could see what was going on up front.

That Sunday morning I found myself watching him. In fact I was absorbed with watching him. He was oblivious to anything else, completely absorbed in the music. His mouth was moving, and though I couldn't hear the sound, I knew he was singing. I knew because when the song ended, and the music stopped, he didn't. His voice carried on as though he was alone in the sanctuary. No matter that he didn't know the words, He knew what his heart wanted to say. The praise rang out and filled the air.

His daddy must have stopped him because the song suddenly ended. I wanted to reach out and say, "Let him sing." But I didn't. I heard perfect praise that day in the sanctuary. And I know that God looked down and smiled.

"From infancy you have known the
Holy Scriptures, which are able to make

you wise for salvation through faith in Christ Jesus" (2 Timothy 3:15).

Luke 19 tells the story of Jesus's triumphal entry into Jerusalem, and about the crowd "coming near the place where the road goes down the Mount of Olives… There the whole crowd of disciples began joyfully to praise God in loud voices for all the miracles they had seen…(v. 37). Some of the Pharisees in the crowd said to Jesus, "'Teacher, rebuke Your disciples!' (v. 39) 'I tell you,' He replied, 'If they keep quiet, the stones will cry out'" (v.40).

How could they keep quiet! Here is the Savior of the world, the Redeemer, the Lamb of God. We will praise Him as long as we have breath!

Here are some suggestions that might help us move out of our timidity, our caution, our negativity, our false humility, and into the presence of God with freedom and the assurance of acceptance:

I.   Bible Reading

The Word of God is a delight to read—a fountain bubbling up onto thirsty ground (Isaiah 35:7). "It is a lamp to my feet and a light for my path" (Psalm 119:105).

That one chapter alone (119) has a treasure chest of words to describe the Bible. They include the law (twenty-four times), testimonies (twenty-four times), precepts (twenty times), statutes (twenty-two times), commandments (twenty-two times), word (forty times), ordinances (sixteen times), ways (one time), and judgments (three times). Read it over and over every day. You will learn to love the Word of God and delight in it as precious jewels.

"How can a young man keep his way pure? By living according to Your Word" (Psalm 119:99). "I have hidden Your Word in my heart that I might not sin against You" (v. 11). "Oh, how I love Your Law! I meditate on it all day long" (v. 97). "The entrance of Your Words gives light" (v. 130).

In reading my Bible, I try not to just skim over the text but look for little things, intriguing things, unusual things that make me want to look further:

a. I try to keep an eye open for what I might normally miss, which could change the whole picture. For instance, find the *He said/he said*, which keeps the dialogue correct. Sometimes it's hard to tell who is speaking otherwise. (It helps to have a Bible in which all names for deity, including pronouns, are capitalized.)

b. Notice the *if/then* couplets and others in your reading, to see what will happen when someone chooses to disobey or make other choices, whether right or wrong.

c. Once I found the words "Who knows?" in the book of Esther and looked for more in the Bible. There are at least three more, which prepare the reader for awesome stories of God's working in the lives of ordinary people.

d. It's interesting to note in the book of Exodus the places God saved His people *with a powerful hand* and/or *with an outstretched arm.*

e. In the book of Mark, I counted the number of times the word *immediately* showed up. It made me start thinking about the author. Who is this man? What do I know about him? Why is everything happening instantly?

I have learned not to be afraid to write in my Bible. It is my workbook. My study book. "Study to show yourself approved unto God, a workman that needeth not to be ashamed, rightly dividing the Word of truth" (2 Timothy 2:15, KJV). I tend to circle or underline words or phrases that have special meaning at the moment. Some people put a date by a verse that seemed exactly right for the situation they are in. If I don't trust myself to place the date and the situation together in my mind later, I could write the date and the occasion in my journal. That way I can check later for the reason I have dated my Bible, sort of a double-check.

Another thing I enjoy is to make an object lesson to help me remember. For instance:

Trace around both hands on a sheet of paper
The first hand will portray *1 Corinthians 16:13*

Starting with the thumb, write one phrase on each finger:

Be on the alert,
Stand firm in the faith,
Be a woman/man of courage,
Be strong,
Do everything in love.

The other hand is *Zephaniah 3:17*
Thumb: The Lord your God is with
you,
He is mighty to save,
He will take great delight in you,
He will quiet you with His love,
He will rejoice over you with singing.

Memorize these, and you have a great start at having something that will help you in any situation.

Read your Bible over and over, week after week, month after month, year after year. Feed on God's Word as with choice food. Now, after nearly fifty times through the Bible, I have just begun to understand sections of Scripture, while remembering other verses that might tie in with what I'm reading today.

An excuse for not rereading the Bible time after time is that it becomes too routine, too familiar, too predictable. But what about the children in our lives? Is time spent with the little ones in our households too predictable, too familiar, too routine? Any number of us would say that nothing is routine or predictable about a child. They are always changing, always needing to be understood in a new way.

What is in God's Word? What is He saying to me this time? I have read this passage so many times I practically have it memorized. Can I summarize to someone else what I read? Was there anything that surprised me? Something I never saw before? God's Word is not stale. It is "living and active. Sharper than any double-edged sword it penetrates even to dividing soul and spirit, joints and marrow; it judges the thoughts and attitudes of the heart" (Hebrews 4:12).

II.   Music

The chief end of all music is the glory of
God and the refreshment of the soul.
                                        —J. S. Bach

I trust in your unfailing love;
My heart rejoices in your salvation.
I will sing to the Lord
For He has been good to
me. (Psalm 13:5–6)

"I will sing of the Lord's great love forever; with my mouth I will make Your faithfulness known through all generations" (Psalm 89:1). "It is good to praise the Lord and to make music to Your name O Most High" (Psalm 92:1). "I sing for joy at the works of Your hands" (Psalm 92:4).

Through all the years of our growing up, we sang. My sisters and I were a trio. My brother was a soloist and quartet member. I actually sang a duet with my dad at a New Years' Eve service when I was in high school. He had a very nice voice, and I enjoyed seeing the look of surprise on everyone's face.

Mostly I played piano for church services, for choir, and for special music. I can claim that I also played the organ, but I better explain! When our family lived in Denver, our whole family helped start a new church. Dad and Mom were more involved than us four teens, but I was invited to play the most unique organ ever.

It was carried like a suitcase into the house where we were to have the service. Then it was unfolded much like a suitcase and set up with two pump pedals hanging below the three-octave keyboard. My job was to sit at the organ, both feet on the pedals and start pumping. The purpose was to keep the music going, and it went fine if I kept both feet and fingers going at the same time. Once in a while I forgot to pedal and found that the keys are no good at that point! It was great fun! I was rather sad when the pastor's family moved into the house, along with their upright piano.

When I was in nursing school in Minnesota, a dear friend was getting married and asked me to play organ for her wedding. The nurses' dorm had a small organ, not at all like the one I would be playing at the church, but it's what there was, so that was where I practiced! I can feel my excitement and embarrassment to this day. But my friend was very lost in her love anyway, so I could have played the suitcase-pumper-pedals organ, and she wouldn't have noticed!

Music has always been a great source of pleasure to me, as well as an instrument of worship. With much time on my hands these days, I am able to spend up to an hour every day just sitting at the piano, playing hymns, fun songs, worship songs, classical. It is a joy and a privilege. I am able to sing and play unto the Lord in worship with no one to bother.

When I got to Chefoo School in Malaysia, I had many opportunities for helping in the music department. Many of the parents wanted their children to learn piano, so I was able to teach several students during the school day. It was a boarding school, so the difficulty was in calling the children in from a ball game or their other play to practice after classes were over for the day!

The fifth and sixth graders were required to be in the school choir and most enjoyed it, so that made it fun. We did at least one full concert every term, including performing *The Sound of Music* one spring.

Recently I was reminded of a fact that I tend to forget: listening, not only playing an instrument or singing, is a vital part of worship. This includes listening to praise and worship songs that are prevalent in many evangelical churches and gospel radio. The words are often taken straight from Scripture and cause us to focus on God in worship and praise. This was brought to my attention a few years ago when a dear couple was looking to fulfill the longing of their hearts for a child and adopt a baby. The process was proceeding when it was interrupted by a change of heart. My friends had to leave empty-handed, crying to God for understanding and help. In the car they turned on a tape of worship music and soaked up God's strength for the journey ahead. In their acceptance, God brought peace and also worked a miracle in the return of the infant.

Praise the Lord with the harp; make music to him on the ten-stringed lyre. (Psalm 33:2)

III.   Prayer

In Exodus 29–31, "There I will meet with you to speak to you" is written three times in the midst of God's instructions to Moses regarding the priesthood and the incense Aaron and his sons were to bring to the altar. When we come to God in prayer, He meets us there. The Holy God comes to speak with us to speak to us

- at the doorway of the tent of meeting before the Lord (Genesis 29:42),
- in front of the mercy seat that is over the ark of the testimony (Genesis 30:6),
- before the testimony in the tent of meeting (Genesis 30:36).

"Since we have confidence to enter the Most Holy Place by the blood of Jesus, by a new and living way opened for us through the curtain, that is, His body, and since we have a great priest over the house of God, let us draw near to God with a sincere heart in full assurance of faith…" (Hebrews 10:19–22).

We worship a Holy God, and often our worship finds us standing still, seeing what is around us, hearing sweet bird songs. My daughter has always had a gift for noticing the little things that matter. One day, standing on the patio on a particularly calm day, she was enjoying the sun and the beauty of fall. After a few minutes she came into the kitchen with her face glowing and her eyes full of wonder. "I can hear the leaves falling!"

And the joy we share as we tarry
there, none other has ever known.
—Charles A. Miles

What a precious time of fellowship this can be—with the Lord Himself. For some it is difficult to find a place to be alone or, at minimum, to have a moment of quiet in a busy household. Where we meet Him is not important. There were often crowds, thousands at a time, around Jesus so that He could not find a quiet place to be alone. "One of those days Jesus went out into the hills to pray, and spent the night praying to God. When morning came, He called

His disciples to Him, and chose twelve of them, whom He also designated apostles" (Mark 3:13, 14).

Jesus, the Son of God, needed time to pray. His fellowship with the Father was critical (extremely important) to Him. How much more should I long for that sweet fellowship and how much more I am dependent on my time alone with our Heavenly Father.

A. Get in a quiet place—Perhaps, like the mother of hymn-writers John and Charles Wesley, the only place I have is under an apron I have thrown over my head. Her eighteen children knew that Mama was not to be disturbed then because she was praying.

B. Quiet my heart—Stand somewhere out of the buzz and ruckus going on around me and breathe in the peace that God promises. Shut my eyes for a brief moment and know that He is God.

He calls me "Beloved"
I call Him LORD.

C. Quiet my mind—In 1 Kings 19, Elijah had been very zealous for the Lord. He had done what God asked him to do, but he was exhausted. He was afraid. When God came to him, He spoke in a powerful wind, an earthquake, and fire. But only when He spoke in a gentle whisper was Elijah able to hear. Before that he was too stressed, wound up too tightly, unable to be silent.

D. Always pray *Thy will be done*—In 2 Samuel 24, King David, in going against God's Word, chose to take a census of fighting-age men in Israel. The command to "count" was "repulsive to Joab and evil in the sight of God, so 70,000 men fell dead because of a plague. And God sent an angel to destroy Jerusalem. But as the angel was doing so, the Lord saw it and was grieved because of the calamity," and commanded the angel to stop. "Enough! Withdraw your hand" (v. 16).

Did God change His mind? No! He is unchangeable and doesn't change His mind, but sometimes His plan of action in response to true repentance and confession of sin. He already knew what would happen and kept His promise of forgiveness.

E. Pray for my family—"We Your people, the sheep of Your pasture, will praise You forever; from generation to generation we will recount Your praise" (Psalm 79:13).

"We will tell the next generation the praiseworthy deeds of the Lord, His power, and the wonders He has done... so the next generation would know them, even the children yet to be born, and they in turn would tell their children. Then they would put their trust in God" (Psalm 78:4).

In my life, God brings about miracles as well in answers to my prayers for my family and for other requests I bring to Him. While I wait, I hope.

If we hope for what we do not yet have, then do we with patience wait for it. We do not know what we ought to pray, but the Spirit intercedes for us in accordance with God's will. (Romans 8:25–27)

F. Prayer doesn't have to be audible: "Before I had finished speaking in my heart, behold Rebekah came out with her jar on her shoulder" (Genesis 24:15).

G. Pray specifically: In Mark 10, "A blind man...was sitting by the roadside begging. When he heard that it was Jesus of Nazareth (walking by), he began to shout, 'Jesus, Son of David, have mercy on me!' Jesus stopped and said, 'Call him.' So they called to the blind man, 'Cheer up! On your feet! He's calling you.' Throwing his cloak aside, he jumped to his feet and came to Jesus. 'What do you want me to do for you?' Jesus asked him. The blind man said, 'Rabbi, I want to see.' And he immediately received his sight."

What might be hindering me from asking for what I need? Is it pride, feeling unworthy, or something more? Hebrews 12:1–5 offers help: *"Let us fix our eyes on Jesus... so that (we) will not grow weary and lose heart. Let us throw off everything that hinders and the sin that so easily entangles, and let us run with perseverance the race marked out for us."*

Prayer is not always easy. I often have trouble sticking with it or knowing what to say. This thought came to me one day: *My Father knows what I need before I ask Him. So stop fretting about using the right words when you pray!* "The Spirit helps us in our weakness. We do not know what we ought to pray, but the Spirit Himself intercedes for us with groans that words cannot express... (Romans 8:26). The Spirit intercedes for the saints in accordance with God's will" (v. 27).

"Christ Jesus, Who died—more than that, Who was raised to life—is at the right hand of God and is also interceding for us" (Romans 8:34). "Call to Me and I will answer you, and tell you great and unsearchable things you do not know" (Jeremiah 33:3).

"The fearful heart will know and understand, and the stammering tongue will be fluent and clear" (Isaiah 32:4).

We mutter and sputter
We fume and we spurt
We mumble and grumble
Our feelings get hurt;
We can't understand things
Our vision grows dim
When all that we need
Is a moment with Him.
—Author Unknown

H. Distractions when praying: I have a dark burgundy robe that I put on when I first get upon cold mornings. It is very soft and warm and is my cat's go-to place to sleep on a cold night. That's all well and good except when I am trying to pray. That robe becomes a number one distraction until I pick off every single crumb, piece of lint, cat hair, anything white or light colored. This means I have been trying to pray with my eyes open, which does not work anyway. Only when I pray audibly, out loud or whispered, with my eyes shut can I keep my mind on my prayer.

Other distractions:

- The phone (turn it off)
- My mind elsewhere (keep a pen and paper handy and write down everything I'm afraid I'll forget when I'm done praying)

- Know that God understands the thoughts of my heart and "the Spirit intercedes for the saints in accordance with God's will" (Romans 8:26–27).

Above all, "Do not be in a hurry to leave the King's presence" (Ecclesiastes 8:3).

God sometimes answers our prayers by
giving us what we would have asked for
had we known what He knows.
—J. D. Greear

IV.   Giving

Be openhanded with what God gives.

In 2 Corinthians 8, Paul wrote to the church in Corinth, along with all the saints throughout Achaia, to tell them what had happened in Macedonia. The churches there suffered "the most severe trial" and yet gave generously to the saints.

> v. 2—Their overflowing joy and extreme poverty welled up in rich generosity.
> v. 3—They gave as much as they were able, and even beyond their ability.
> v. 4—They urgently pleaded with us for the privilege of sharing in this service to the saints.

v. 5—They gave themselves first to the Lord.

v. 9—"You know the grace of our Lord Jesus Christ, that though He was rich, yet for your sakes He became poor…"

v. 12—"If the willingness is there, the gift is acceptable according to what one has, no according to what he does not have."

"Give and it will be given to you. A good measure, pressed down, shaken together and running over, will be poured into your lap. For with the measure you use, it will be measured to you" (Luke 6:38).

The Lord said to (Moses), "What is that in your hand?" "A staff," he replied (Exodus 4:2).

Whatever it is, God can use it.

Giving is most often taken to mean monetary gifts, but includes so much more:

Your time—children's Sunday school teacher or helper, adult teacher, Bible study leader, life group leader, prayer group leader, library staff, youth group leader, mentor, nursery worker, jail ministry, prayer chain, city mission, missionary correspondence, pregnancy center volunteer

Your talent—musical instrument, vocal group, ministry leader, preaching, Elder, deacon, office staff, church secretary, janitorial staff, kitchen crew, meal delivery

Little is much when God is in it.
Labor not for wealth or fame;
There's a crown, and you can win it
If you go in Jesus' name.
                    —Kittie Louise Suffield

NOW WHAT?

On reaching eighty I find that I'm not alone. I have lots of company! Several friends, family members, church leaders, plenty famous men and women have joined the ranks of the octogenarian. In our town I have noticed a definite dearth of pretty, uplifting greeting cards that say "Happy 80th Birthday" because I have bought them out! The year 1939 turned out to be a happy year for births in the Midwestern United States.

None of us have the history that Moses had. By the time he was eighty years old he could write a book! All he needed was a quill and ink, along with fresh papyrus reeds for paper. Born to a Hebrew couple (Amram and Jochebed), he spent his first three months in hiding, then in a basket floating on the Nile River. He had lived in a palace, was wanted for murder, escaped into the wilderness, herded sheep, spoken to God in a bush that was burning, married a priest's daughter, and had two sons. At that point he was charged by God, along with his brother Aaron, with the mission of leading His people to freedom, over a million people in fact. And that was just the first eighty years.

Then began book two! "So Moses and Aaron did it; as the Lord commanded them, thus they did. Moses was eighty years old and Aaron eighty-three, when they spoke to Pharaoh" (Exodus 7:6, 7). They went to see Pharaoh just as the Lord commanded. And they spoke just what the Lord commanded. *Pharaoh, let my people go.* That was their *purpose* at that time.

In Deuteronomy 29:5 Moses told the people, "I have led you forty years in the wilderness," and went on to remind the people all that God had done for them. By now Moses is 120 years old. Even then he led the people in a song that he wrote for the occasion (Exodus 15:1–2).

I will sing to the Lord
For He is highly exalted;
The horse and its rider
He has hurled into the sea.
The Lord is my strength
and song,
And He has become
my salvation;
This is my God,
and I will praise Him.

(Read the rest of his
song in Exodus 15)

In the Old Testament, and especially in the days before the Exodus, men lived to an old age, in fact *very* old age (maybe women too, but the Bible doesn't tell us their age. God withholds some things in His wisdom). A couple exceptions include Abraham's wife, Sarah, who had a baby when she was 91 and lived to be 127 years old (Genesis 23:1, NASB). Then there was the prophetess, Anna, who the Bible called "very old." She lived with her husband seven years after her marriage and then was a widow until she was eighty-four. She never left the temple but worshipped night and day while waiting for the promised redeemer (Luke 2:36–38).

Also Elizabeth, the mother of John the Baptist. The Bible doesn't give her age but alludes to it when she is listed as *barren*. Also she and her husband Zacharias were *well along in years*. But Luke gives this exciting report: The angel to Mary, "Even Elizabeth your relative is going to have a child in her old age, and she who was said to be barren is in her sixth month. For nothing is impossible with God" (Luke 1:36–37). I can just hear him throwing in a rousing "Hallelujah!"

When the Bible talks about old age, it doesn't always say those words but uses adjectives, descriptions, symptoms of the aged one, plus some directions and joyous *Amens*.

- Jacob: old man, and a young son of his old age (Genesis 44:20)
- Jacob: years of his life were 147…(47:28)
- Jacob: when I rest with my fathers, carry me out of Egypt (v.30)
- Israel: eyes dim for age (Genesis 48:10)
- Joseph: old and well advanced in years (Joshua 23:1)
- Gideon: a ripe old age (Judges 8:32)
- Jesse: old and well advanced in years (1 Samuel 17:12)

- Barzillai: very old, being eighty years old! (2 Samuel 19:32)
- Eli: was ninety-eight years old, his eyes were set so that he could not see (2 Samuel 4:15)
- Ahijah: his sight was gone because of his age (1 Kings 14:4)
- David: a good old age (1 Chronicles 29:28)
- Jehoiada: old and full of years (2 Chronicles 24:15)
- Paul: I appeal to you as an old man (Philippians 9)

Were these people all serving God's purpose, even in their old age? Absolutely! God doesn't need us to be perfect. We simply need to be available and willing.

What are the *promises* given to us in our older years:

- "My age is as nothing before Thee" (Psalm 39:5). "It is nothing with thee to help" (2 Chronicles 14:11, KJV). It doesn't matter how old I am or how weak or strong. It is not about God's ability or desire to help or care for us as we age. He is *always* able, *always* waiting for us to call.
- (He) satisfies your years with good things, so that your youth is renewed like the eagle" (Psalm 103:5, NASB).
- "Even to your old age and gray hairs I am He, I am He who will sustain you" (Isaiah 46:4).
- "Precious in the sight of the Lord is the death of His saints" (Psalm 15:16).
- "Know therefore that the Lord your God, He is God, the faithful God, who keeps His covenant and His loving-kindness to a thousandth genera-

tion with those who love Him and keep His commandments" (Deuteronomy 7:9).

- "They will still bear fruit in old age, they will stay fresh and green" (Psalm 92:14).

And my dependence on these promises:

- "Do not cast me off in the time of old age" (Psalm 71:9).
- "Even when I am old and gray, do not forsake me. O God, till I declare Your power to the next generation, Your might to all who are to come" (Psalm 71:18).
- "I have been young and now I am old, yet I have not seen the righteous forsaken or his descendants begging bread. All day long he is gracious and lends, and his descendants are a blessing" (Psalm 37:25, 26).
- "Your word, O Lord, is eternal; it stands firm in the heavens. Your faithfulness continues through all generations" (Psalm 119:90).
- "Your statutes are my heritage forever; they are the joy of my heart. My heart is set on keeping your decrees to the very end" (Psalm 119:111, 112).

The man who trusts in the Lord...
never fails to bear fruit. (Jeremiah 17:8)

Closing Thoughts

"Stand at the crossroads and look; ask for the ancient paths, ask where the good way is and walk in it, and you will find rest for your souls" (Jeremiah 6:16).

"We will tell the next generation the praiseworthy deeds of the Lord, His power, and the wonders He has done. He decreed statutes for Jacob and established the law in Israel, which He commanded our forefathers to teach their children, so the next generation would know them, even the children yet to be born, and they in turn would tell their children. Then they would put their trust in God" (Psalm 78:4–7).

What's the end that God
has set in all His ways?
Surely, it is that His blessed
name be magnified,
that His glory may be set forth.

Then that shall be the great
design of my life.
—Jeremiah Burroughs[*]

---

[*] Jeremiah Burroughs, *A Life of Gospel Peace* (Reformation Heritage Books) 2011.

REFERENCES

All Scripture quotations from the New International Version, unless otherwise stated.

Scripture taken from the Holy Bible, New International Version, copyright 1973, 1978, 1984, Int'l Bible Society, Used by permission of Zondervan Bible Publishers.

Scripture taken from the New American Standard Bible, Copyright 1960, 1962, 1963, 1968, 1971, 1972, 1973, 1975, 1977, 1995 by the Lockman Foundation. Used by permission.

Dictionary used is *Webster's New Collegiate Dictionary*, G. & C. Merriam Co, 1958.

CPSIA information can be obtained
at www.ICGtesting.com
Printed in the USA
FSHW011649030221
78215FS

9 781098 040673